The **Parent** Guide to the Toddler Years

The **Parent**alk Guide to the Toddler Years

Steve Chalke

Hodder & Stoughton
LONDON SYDNEY AUCKLAND

British Library Cataloguing in Publication Data
A record for this book is available from the British Library

ISBN 0 340 72167 7

Typeset in Monotype Sabon by
Strathmore Publishing Services, London N7

Printed and bound in Great Britain by
Clays Ltd, St Ives PLC

Hodder and Stoughton
A division of Hodder Headline Ltd
338 Euston Road
London NW1 3BH

CONTENTS

Foreword   vii

Introduction   1

Part One: Firm Foundations

1 A Lifetime's Investment
How Can I Survive Living with a Toddler?   3

2 'I've Pencilled In Your Bedtime Story for Next Week'
How Can I Make Time for My Toddler?   21

3 'But Of Course I Do'
How Can I Show My Toddler I Love Them?   39

Part Two: First Steps

4 'If You Don't Stop Crying,
I'll Give You Something to Cry About!'
How Do I Discipline My Toddler?   55

5 Last in the Class
What If My toddler Is … ?   85

6 An Awfully Big Adventure
How Can I Make Learning Fun?   112

Part Three: The Big Wide World

7 'A Real Social Climber'
  How Do I Teach My Toddler to Get On with Others?   136

8 'Well, He Started It!'
  How Do I Cope with Jealousy and Sibling Rivalry?   150

9 'There's No Place Like Home'
  An A to Z of Toddler Troubleshooting   160

The Last Word   176

Further Information   179

FOREWORD

'Leave it, Jack. No, Jack. NO, Jaaack! Jaaaack! Nooooooooooooo!'

I was a nanosecond too late. My fourteen-month-old son had pulled a stack of cereal bowls (wedding presents, I might add) from the kitchen cupboard onto the tiled kitchen floor. The 'child proof' safety catch that I had spent hours fitting had failed to do its job and Jack found himself surrounded by hundreds of sharp china pieces.

This, of course, is just one snapshot of my life as the father of a toddler. There's also been the systematic chewing of my CD and record collection, the sitting up half the night watching *Teletubbies* videos because Jack has decided he's not in the least bit tired any more and no one else should be either, and the inevitable had-to-change-my-shirt-three-times-this-morning-already routine because Jack had Weetabix for breakfast.

All these scenes of devastation pale into insignificance, however, whenever Jack says a new word, or I catch his eye across a room, when he breaks into that toothy grin of his, or even when he just needs a cuddle and comes to me to provide it.

The truth is, I love Jack – I love him so much it hurts – but I am still very much *learning* how to cope with him and be a good father to him. And to be honest, I need all the help I can get! That's what *The Parentalk Guide to the Toddler Years* is all about – not giving foolproof suggestions on every parenting issue (because they don't exist!), but providing a gold mine of helpful hints and practical advice for plodding parents like me.

I hope you enjoy reading this book. But more importantly, I hope you find it encouraging and reassuring in your role as a parent. The toddler years are a massive challenge but fabulously rewarding as well – let's make the most of them.

Tim Mungeam
Chief Executive, **Parentalk**
LONDON, *January 1999*

INTRODUCTION

Being a parent is, at one and the same time, the most wonderful privilege and the most daunting challenge of your life. This 'small task' will stretch you more than anything you've attempted before … and probably more than anything you'll ever face in the future. But for those who're willing to put in the effort, it can also be the most exciting, rewarding and fulfilling experience of your life!

If you're anything like me, there's a nagging feeling at the back of your mind that everyone else is doing a better job of being a parent than you are. But the truth is, they're not. We all make mistakes. None of us is perfect. We all do and say things that, with hindsight, we wish we hadn't.

In over fifteen years of dealing with family problems – both personally and professionally – I've come across very few parents who have any real confidence in their ability to do a good job. Though most mums and dads actually do an *excellent* job, they fall into the trap of measuring their performance against totally unrealistic 'ideals', and then feel inadequate when they can't match up.

The fact of the matter is, you'll never be a *perfect* parent. But not only can you be a good parent, you can even be a *great* parent – one your child is really proud of. And to achieve it, all you need are the three essential qualities available to every mum or dad whatever their situation in life: love, time and a little bit of self-trust.

1

Families aren't standard issue. They come in all shapes and sizes – not just the classic Hollywood version of mum, dad, two kids and a dog. There are models with one child and those with six – even those where all six were born together! There are those where the children, or some of them, have been adopted, and those where one is physically disabled or has a learning disability. And, for all sorts of reasons, there are those with just one parent – sometimes a mum, sometimes a dad. Sometimes there's a step-parent and step-children. But whatever your family looks like, this book is for you.

There are, of course, many reasons why you might be reading it: you may simply be looking for reassurance that what you're doing as a mum or dad is along the right lines; or you may need urgent help. Perhaps your child is in some kind of trouble, and you want to know what to do about it.

This book is about the basic principles and skills that every parent, regardless of their individual circumstances, needs in order not only to *survive* being a parent, but to *thrive*. But be warned: they're *not* short-cuts. They all require effort. The reason for this is simple: short-cuts just don't work.

So read on, because the relationship that any child has with their parent is the most formative and influential one of their lives. That's why my hope and sincere prayer is that this book serves you well.

PART ONE: FIRM FOUNDATIONS

A Lifetime's Investment

How Can I Survive Living with a Toddler?

'That's one small step for a man, one giant leap for mankind.' These words were spoken by Neil Armstrong as he became the first man ever to set foot on the moon on 20 July 1969. And they were the words that sprang to mind as I watched my elder daughter Emily take her first steps. Though she managed just a few hesitant paces across the room – grinning, gurgling and giggling – before plopping down on her bottom as her balance and nerve suddenly deserted her, I knew that a whole new chapter was beginning in the history of the Chalke family. And though the entire experience lasted just a few seconds, the sense of pride and joy I felt then will stay with me for ever. Emily was walking, but *I* was flying!

Looking back, our four children's 'toddler years' are brimful of wonderful memories. Cornelia, my wife, still says they were some of the best days of all. In her capacity as a 'domestic engineer' (otherwise known as a full-time mum), she spent almost every waking moment for the better part of a decade surrounded by Junior Rambos hell-bent on causing havoc – and says she loved every minute of it! Well, hindsight is a marvellous thing!

WHERE DO TODDLERS GET THEIR ENERGY FROM?

PROBABLY FROM US- I CERTAINLY HAVEN'T GOT ANY LEFT...

But the truth is that being a mum or dad to a toddler *is* a wonderful and totally unique experience. The whole period – from the time they first start not just crawling but walking around, to the time you pack them off to primary school as a 'rising five' – has a marvellous, magical quality to it. Toddlerhood is a thrilling voyage of discovery for both parent and child. And though every stage of a child's development holds exciting treasures in store for any parent who makes it a priority to get involved, there's nothing quite like these extraordinary first years.

Top Tip: *Being a parent to a toddler is an amazing, unparalleled experience – it just happens to be a rather exhausting one as well!*

And Now for Something Completely Different …

But as well as being a fun-filled, fantastic experience, being a toddler's mum or dad can be a bit – well, difficult. In fact, it's a heart-thumping, blood-pumping, stomach-tightening, knuckle-whitening rollercoaster of a ride. It's every bit as exciting as it is frightening. And vice versa. And nothing can adequately prepare you for its impact.

> **toddler** *n.* **1** very small person with a disproportionate ratio of energy to common sense. **2** fun-filled creature characterised by non-stop activity, requiring constant attention but able to create extreme pleasure in those around them. **3** miniature demolitions expert. **4** stubborn, selfish, jealous, competitive and extremely emotionally sensitive terrorist.

Obviously before Cornelia and I became parents, we knew *exactly* what to expect. We'd made a very close inspection of how our friends and relations brought up their children. We'd carefully noted their mistakes and would smile at each other knowingly as we watched their faltering efforts. We knew how it *should* be done. We'd never shout at, smack, spoil or bribe our children, or sit them in front of the TV just to shut them up. *Our* kids would never misbehave at table, throw food, pick their nose or fight. Instead, they'd

5

be polite, thoughtful, well-behaved and sweet-natured. We knew just what to expect and how to cope. We belonged to the breed of parents who had it sorted.

And then – we had Emily. Suddenly the truth hit us like a freight train: the only people who're certain about exactly how to raise children are those who've never had any! Only *they* can maintain the kind of naive, know-it-all 'expertise' that any parent has had knocked out of them by experience. Before we had our first child, we were proud of our carefully developed 'Ten Commandments' on how to raise a happy family. But by the time Emily was a year old, we'd downgraded them to 'Ten Handy Hints', and within another six months we'd abandoned them altogether. As the saying goes, 'I used to have four theories on child-rearing and no kids. Now I've got four kids and no theories!'

Preparing for Life with a Toddler: A Beginner's Guide

1 Smear and flick a mixture of peanut butter and jam over all the tables, chairs, doors and other furniture in your house.

2 Pour Ribena over the carpet, and douse important documents liberally with honey or other sticky substances.

3 Draw all over the walls at knee height with different coloured crayons – beginning with the rooms you've decorated most recently.

4 Stuff bits of Lego, paper, crayon or toy soldiers into the toaster, video recorder and any other items of sensitive electrical equipment you have in the house.

---

5 Stop reading a newspaper and watching the TV (except for daily doses of *Postman Pat* and the *Teletubbies*, played on a continuous loop).

6 Programme your CD player to come on at full volume at six every morning, including weekends and bank holidays.

7 Buy a copy of *Where's Spot?* and read it ten times a day for a whole week, making sure you maintain an equally high level of enthusiasm on each reading.

8 Arrange for an insensitive friend to barge in, sit down and refuse to leave whenever you've planned a romantic evening.

9 Paint the dog/cat/rabbit/hamster fluorescent green.

10 Tip the entire contents of your wallet into the bin.

Life is cruel. Just when you're coming to terms with the joy of being a new parent, your baby gets up and starts walking around – and the world you once knew abruptly ceases to exist. Having finally got used to the routine of a new baby, there are suddenly all sorts of new dangers and challenges, and you're not really sure *what* to expect any more. Except chaos.

I remember one occasion when some friends called round to see us, bringing their two toddler daughters with them. It was great to see them, and I was really looking forward to spending the day with them. Emily was still a baby, and after about six months of adjusting to her needs and routine, I'd finally begun to build up a bit of self-confidence as a dad. I was even looking forward to getting a 'sneak preview' of the joys we had to come when Emily went mobile on us. But nothing could have prepared me for what was about to happen to the relative peace and quiet of our front room.

In the space of twenty minutes, every trace of the parental confidence I'd slowly gained was destroyed. I sat on the sofa, paralysed with fear and panic. I couldn't believe that two such small creatures – a two-year-old and a three-year-old – could be responsible for so much noise, chaos and devastation. They behaved just like unguided missiles, packed with explosive power and completely unpredictable. They appeared to be utterly devoid of any self-control or any glimmer of common sense. It was agony to watch as their parents stoically struggled against the odds to create and maintain some semblance of order for more than two minutes at a stretch. How did they cope? And how would *I* cope when, in just a few short months, Emily joined this manic world of mobile madness?

The truth is, every parent experiences this form of panic in one way or another, so try not to imagine you must be doing something wrong just because your world has suddenly and dramatically been turned upside down. The 'toddler tornado' will wreak havoc on your life, home, car and anything and everything in its path! It seems crass to say 'Don't worry', but it's true. It's a normal part of bringing up a child, and it *is* survivable!

Top Tip: *However ready you think you are, you'll never be fully prepared for a toddler!*

Nature vs Nurture: The Championship Bout

Being a mum or dad is a wonderful experience, but it's also a big responsibility. What we do today as parents has a huge impact on what our children become in the future. We have a great deal of influence on their lives. And since they'll probably have kids of their own, the way we perform will have a big impact on the next generation as well.

During toddlerhood, children develop the foundations of their personality and temperament. Although some aspects of their personality, like their physical appearance, are a result of their genes, many more are slowly determined by the way they respond to their environment – in other words, by their circumstances and the choices they make. Each of us is a product of both 'nature' and 'nurture'. There's not much you can do about nature any more, but there's a lot you can do to nurture your toddler. As a mum or dad, you have a huge level of control over their circumstances – what happens to them and how they're treated – as well as being their main guide when it comes to making choices. This means you have a massive influence on the kind of person your toddler grows up to be. To a large extent, every child is 'home made', and – along with a partner if you have one – *you* create the home.

The lessons your toddler learns from you, and the level of

9

support and attention you give them, will work for or against them later in life. The more time and tenderness you're willing to invest in them in these vital formative years, the easier you'll make it for yourself later on, and the more chance you'll give them to grow into a happy, mature, self-confident adult. It's a heavy investment to make, but the dividends it'll pay to you and your toddler in years to come make it worth every penny!

Top Tip: *You can't do anything about your toddler's genes, but you can do a lot to control their circumstances and guide their choices.*

Great Expectations

But what makes this *Mission Impossible* really daunting is the total lack of real experience that any new parent has. At least Jim Phelps, the team leader in the famous TV series, could rely on seasoned experts to help him get the job done. His team never failed in its 'mission impossible' because everyone knew just what they were doing. But new parents have *no* idea what they're doing, *no* guarantee that they're following the right tactics, and *no* certainty that it'll succeed. In short, they start their mission with no preparation, no rehearsal and no plan.

Normally, before we have to do anything important in our lives, we get the chance to prepare ourselves for it in advance. Exams, driving tests, playing in the school concert – whatever it is, we rehearse it carefully beforehand. For couples who get married in church, there's often even a walk-through rehearsal the day before the wedding to ensure they know where they're supposed to stand, what they're supposed to say, and when they're supposed to say it. But when it comes to being a parent, there's *nothing*. You're suddenly thrown in at the deep end without a life jacket.

When Emily was a small baby, Corni and I were worried because she'd started sleeping right through the night – a full eight hours. Now most couples would thank God for sending them so 'considerate' a child, but not us. With no experience to fall back on, we became convinced there was something wrong. We got so worried that we used to go into her room in the middle of the night and deliberately wake her up, just to check that she wasn't hungry! Looking back now it seems ridiculous, but at the time we were worried that she'd starve if we didn't take action. It's just the kind of thing new parents do, because no one's told them otherwise and they lack the wisdom that comes from experience.

A hundred years ago, families lived in larger units, often with three or four generations together under one roof, so there was always an experienced mum or dad around to help out and show the proud new parents what to do. Nowadays, for a variety of reasons, the family has shrunk, and a parent can be left with the Herculean task of raising several kids on their own, with no outside support whatsoever – and even having to hold down a job at the same time.

It's never been easy raising children. But in spite of all the technological advances that our society has produced, and the sheer number of labour-saving devices now available to parents, I think it's true to say that being a mum or dad has never been tougher than it is today. So don't worry because you're struggling – I don't know a decent mum or dad who doesn't struggle *constantly* with the demands of parenthood. In fact, given the enormity of the task, struggling is 100 per cent normal for a parent. As they say in the army, 'Situation Normal: All Fouled Up'!

> **Top Tip:** Set yourself realistic expectations – don't give yourself a hard time unnecessarily.

Doing What Comes Naturally

We all want to 'put our best foot forward'. We want to give others as good an impression of ourselves as we can. From dressing up for a job interview to big corporations hiring PR consultants to modernise their image and design new logos, the basic desire is exactly the same: to present ourselves in the best possible light.

It's exactly the same when it comes to being a parent. For example, the first thing most of us think of when our toddler throws a tantrum in Tesco's or a sulk in Sainsbury's is, what will everyone think? We convince ourselves that other people's kids are perfectly behaved little angels, and we're the only parents in the world to have given birth to a Mutant Monster Swamp Thing. But the truth is that no toddler is polite, patient, considerate, obedient, self-sacrificing or self-disciplined all the time. Put simply, they're not old enough to have learnt these qualities yet. That's what childhood is *for*!

Don't torture yourself by imagining that everyone else's toddler is better behaved and better adjusted than yours. It simply isn't true. Does your toddler:

- Frequently resist going to bed, and scream when you finally leave them there?
- Fight or quarrel, aggressively, with their brother or sister?
- Display a highly developed sense of selfishness and jealousy?
- Talk back to you cheekily?
- Wet the bed at night whenever you decide to trust them without a nappy?
- Climb everything they can, without the use of a crash helmet and safety line?
- Stubbornly refuse to do what you say, deliberately testing how far they can push you?
- Interrupt you if you're doing something important, especially if you're on the phone?,
- Seek constant attention, almost every minute they're awake?
- Cry at the slightest provocation?
- Often fly into a temper or tantrum, especially when other people are looking?
- Play with everything, giving things a liberal coating of drool?
- Say 'It's mine' about everything in sight?
- Toddle around and talk to 'the world in general' incessantly?
- Undress themselves after you've dressed them, particularly when you're running late?
- Whine, whinge and nag about whatever comes to mind, even if they liked it yesterday?

- Complain about certain types of food, using it to redecorate the floor and walls?
- Cling to you at inconvenient moments, threatening the circulation in your leg?
- Tell you they need the loo just five seconds before the big event?
- Have disturbing dreams or nightmares several times a week?
- Always try to play with the most dangerous thing in the house?
- Chew books, newspapers, magazines and anything made of paper?
- Throw a wobbly if they lose a favourite 'comfort' toy?
- Suck their thumb and pick their nose (even at the same time)?
- Ask the same question over and over again, especially 'why'?
- Sulk whenever they don't get what they want?
- Refuse to share, or wait, or take their turn?
- Imagine there are toddler-munching monsters lurking in the dark?
- Start things, but never quite get round to finishing them?
- Get frustrated or impatient when they can't do something?

If your toddler does any or all of these things, then prepare yourself for a terrible shock: they're 100 per cent normal! There's nothing wrong with them – or you, for that matter. This is natural toddler behaviour. In fact, these are probably the 'Top Thirty' toddler traits (though they're not in any particular order). *Most* toddlers will exhibit *most* of them at some time and to some extent between the ages of one and four.

So banish from your mind the idea that you must be doing something wrong because your 'little terror' seems to hit more of the Top Thirty traits than your friends' or neighbours' children.

Top Tip: *If everyone else's child seems better behaved than yours, you're probably not seeing the whole picture.*

Left Holding the Baby

Your child's toddler years can be one of the most wonderful experiences you'll ever have. They can also be the hardest, most physically and emotionally draining years of your life. We've all heard the expression about someone being 'left holding the baby' when they've been dumped with a mammoth responsibility without adequate preparation, resources or support. Well, when you become a parent, it's *literally* true.

It's easy to forget, in the maelstrom of madness and chaos that a toddler drags in their wake, just how enjoyable being a parent can be – the first time you held your baby in your arms, their first smile, first bath, first word or step, as well as those little everyday things that fill you with a deep sense of joy. But these are moments we must never forget, because they provide the emotional and spiritual 'fuel' that'll keep us going through all the difficult times.

It's vital not just to keep hold of your goal – to help shape a mature, strong, sensitive, self-confident, creative, constructive young person – but also to keep reminding yourself of the incredible privilege of being a mum or dad. Believe it or not, your state of mind plays a big part in helping you achieve your aim. Prophecies of doom and gloom can all too easily become self-fulfilling. The

15

more you convince yourself you *can't* do something, the more likely you are to fail. On the other hand, the more you focus on your strengths and what you *can* achieve, the more likely you are to succeed.

I'm a big Crystal Palace fan, and I've never ceased to be amazed at the difference a new manager or coach can make to a struggling club. After a string of lost games and facing the prospect of imminent relegation to a lower division, a team can nevertheless miraculously turn itself around and display a whole new form simply because of the arrival of a new leader. By boosting morale and confidence levels, a new manager can turn a downward spiral into a winning streak that'll boost morale and confidence even more. To a wavering team, a positive mental attitude can make the difference between winning and losing.

And it's very similar for parents. We've *all* got plenty of mistakes to dwell on if we choose to, but if we do we'll simply end up disheartened and demoralised, and be plunged into a downward spiral. By focusing our minds instead on those wonderful, 'golden moments' of parenthood, it's possible to find the strength and confidence to keep going through even the most traumatic and demanding episodes of toddlerhood.

A good friend of mine ran the famous London Marathon last year. Though he'd trained really hard for it, running several miles almost every day for six months beforehand and completing a couple of half-marathons in the weeks preceding the big event, it was the first time he'd ever run the full twenty-six miles. It was immensely hard work – harder than he'd ever imagined. In fact, just like the other thirty thousand runners, he had moments during the race when he wondered why he was running it at all, and why he didn't just give up. In the end, he says, it was only the thought of the much-needed money he was raising for charity and the encouragement of the crowds that kept him going through the 'pain barrier' to reach the finish line.

Being a parent can often seem like running a marathon. Even though you're surrounded by countless other people doing exactly the same thing, you can feel totally lonely, isolated and exhausted, often unsure whether you've got enough energy and confidence to stay the course. In fact, almost every parent I've ever spoken to feels under-prepared and not up to the task. So here's the good news: the feelings of inadequacy and bewilderment you're experiencing are entirely natural. Everyone has them. You're normal!

Though some parents have a slightly easier time than others, everyone's in pretty much the same situation. So don't believe the myth that there are happy families just down the street, with perfectly behaved toddlers and no real problems where the parents have got it all sorted out and under control. If you could have the advantage of a hidden closed circuit camera, you'd see that, behind their front doors, these families have the same troubles, tensions, squabbles and dilemmas as everyone else. As they say, the grass may be greener 'over there', but it still needs mowing!

 Top Tip: *Feelings of inadequacy and self-doubt are entirely normal, as being a parent is tough.*

The Vital Ingredient

The truth is, you're a *good* parent. I can say this with absolute confidence because – to put it bluntly – uncaring parents don't bother to read books on how to improve their parenting skills. So the very fact that you're reading this book proves you want to be as great a parent as you possibly can be. It's parents who won't listen or who think they've got it all sewn up who're really in trouble.

The truth is, there's no sure-fire way to raise a perfect and happy child. And there's no magic formula, $x+y=mc^2$, that'll solve all your toddler parenting problems. There's not even any guarantee that what works with one toddler one day will work with the same toddler – or any other toddler – the next. Being a parent isn't like an exact science. There are no foolproof methods for achieving your desired result – the kind that never vary, whoever you are, and never fail. Instead, being a parent is more like an art form. The techniques are as individual as the children themselves. There are one or two key principles to learn, like learning scales in order to master the guitar or the piano, and this book will continue to outline those in what I hope will be a practical, readable way. But even once you've mastered these principles, there's no substitute for individual flair and style. Being a great mum or dad entails a lot more than just knowing the basics. Most of the time, it's also a matter of trusting your own judgment and doing it your own way.

If being a parent is life's greatest adventure, it's also its greatest experiment. A lot of the time it comes down to trial and error: unbalanced, unplannable, unpredictable and chaotic. Even having lots of children doesn't qualify someone to give absolute, set-in-stone,

tried and tested, Good-Housekeeping-Seal-of-Approval rules for success, because there just aren't any! Other parents can share what they've learnt from personal experience, and 'experts' like me can outline the basic principles. But no one can give you fail-safe rules for what to do in every situation, because every child is different. So even when you've been doing it for years, you still have to make it up as you go along. Parenting means improvising.

What's more, however long you've been at it, you'll still get frustrated with your own performance. Books and courses can help a lot, but whatever you've heard or read, you can't expect to get it all right from the start. Success in parenting, as in any other area of life, is a result of making good decisions. Good decisions are the result of experience. And experience is the often painful result of learning from your bad decisions. So don't torture yourself with unrealistic expectations of doing a 'perfect' job – which just isn't possible for *anyone*. Instead, try to relax and enjoy being a parent. After all, you're the best mum or dad your toddler could have. So work hard, but above all – trust yourself!

Top Tip: There's no such thing as a 'perfect' parent, but you can be a **great** parent. The vital ingredient is simple – trust yourself.

'I've Pencilled In Your Bedtime Story for Next Week'

How Can I Make Time for My Toddler?

A funny thing happened on my birthday last year. Knowing that I had to leave the house at 7 a.m., my children arranged an early breakfast for me before I set out. They were keen to celebrate, and didn't want to wait until I got home to watch me open the presents they'd bought me. So we all trooped down to the kitchen in the small hours of the morning for my special birthday surprise.

As they'd hoped, it turned out to be an unforgettable occasion – though not for the reasons any of us expected. As we crowded round the kitchen table munching cereal, and I ripped open my presents, Friday (our cat) ran into the room and began sniffing around excitedly. He often does strange things, so we didn't take much notice until he suddenly sprang into action. A mouse darted out from under the table and ran full-pelt across the floor, and Friday pounced. But no sooner had he caught it in his mouth than my wife and several of the children simultaneously let out a deafening shriek. Friday was so startled that he dropped the mouse, which scuttled to safety behind a large cupboard. For the next twenty minutes, until I had to leave, all six of us (seven including Friday) tried – and failed – to catch the mouse. I've already forgotten most of the presents, but none of us will ever forget that birthday. Years from now, we'll still laugh about 'the year of the rodent'.

Shared memories bind families together – and they'll prove to be as valuable to your child in the years ahead as they will be to you. I recently met a mum who sighed whenever she thought about her children's toddler years. 'I wish I could live those years again,' she told me. 'I really loved them. At least I still have the memories.' She looks back on them as a magical time, filled with wonder and excitement. But for her kids, the memories she talks of will be more than that – they'll be crucial in forming the type of person they become.

Childhood memories are powerful things. The more happy memories you have to look back on when you're older, the happier you tend to be about *who* you are as a person. Philippa clearly remembers being packed off to boarding school by her parents when she was five. They had no real choice about sending her: there weren't any English-speaking schools where they were living. Yet though she fully understood this at the time, and knew her parents loved her, she still looks back on that moment and somehow *feels* as if they were rejecting her. The memory, and the feelings it arouses, have made it hard for her to accept it emotionally when friends and relations tell her they love her, even when she *knows* in her mind they do.

Most of us, of course, have few real memories of what we were like as toddlers, though any we do have are firmly etched into our consciousness because they were particularly good or particularly bad. Instead, what we tend to carry with us is an impression of what our early childhood was like. Individual memories merge together in our subconscious, creating an overall image that has a massive impact on our state of mind. If that impression is of being happy and accepted, then we're far more likely to be secure and self-confident as adults than if it's of a tense environment filled with conflict and uncertainty.

This means that the harder you work to make your child's toddlerhood happy, filled with good memories for them to look back on and an overwhelming impression of having been loved, wanted and accepted unconditionally, the easier you make it for them to be happy and secure not only throughout their childhood, but also later as an adult. The problem is, of course, that all this takes time.

> **Top Tip:** The more happy memories your toddler has to look back on, the more likely they are to be happy and secure as an adult.

Spelling Lessons

We all have so many competing demands made on our time that it's usually hard to see how we can fit everything in. The truth is, of course, that we *can't* fit everything in. None of us can do everything we want to, or give time to everything we feel deserves it. So we have to make hard choices. Something has to go.

Most of us know this. The problem is, we often underestimate the amount of time our toddler needs from us, and just how high a priority we need to make spending time with them. A two- or three-year-old doesn't care *why* we have to work such long hours and can't be there to read them a bedtime story, or *why* we have to do so many household chores and can't play with them: all they know is, we're not *there* for them. And they'll inevitably attach just one interpretation to it: they're not important or valuable enough for us to *make* them a high enough priority to be there.

Harold Wilson once quipped, 'A week is a long time in politics.' But for the average toddler, a week can be an eternity. In fact, it's almost 1 per cent of a two-year-old's entire life so far! Toddlers are basically self-centred creatures, with no real sense of perspective yet. That means they're genuinely unable to fathom the long-term consequences of their actions or how they fit into life's overall game plan. They have no sense whatsoever of the wants and needs of other people, including you. For them, everything is immediate, and their only real concern with something is how it affects them *now*.

When a toddler wants you to see something, for example, they want you to see it *right now*. And they don't think twice about interrupting what you're doing. In fact, they don't usually even think *once* about it. They just act. When was the last time you heard a toddler say something like, 'Oh sorry, you're busy, I'll come back later. I was going to show you something, but it'll keep.' To a toddler, nothing keeps. Especially if they're only one or two (rather than three or four), their attention span is so short that things are usually either now or not at all.

Like all children, toddlers spell 'love' T-I-M-E. They judge their self-importance on the *quantity* and *quality* of time we spend with them. This makes a lot of sense, when you think about it. After all, when you love someone, you want to spend as much time with them as you can. Young lovers frequently stay up until the small hours of the morning talking about nothing in particular, just for the sheer pleasure of spending time with the person they love. It's an important way of 'bonding'. And it's just the same for toddlers. The time you spend with them is 'bonding time', reassuring them that you love them and that they're important. Just being around sends them the message, 'I like you. I'm glad you're here.'

Sometimes all that's required is for you to be there in the room while they play on their own. At other times, you'll need to be more actively involved in what they're doing. All toddlers are 'attention junkies', which means you'll often have to stop what you're doing and look at what they're doing instead. The important principle is that it's not enough for you to be paying attention – your toddler has to *know* that you're paying attention.

When I took my driving test, my instructor told me to exaggerate every move I made. 'It's not enough to look in the mirror before you signal, Steve,' he told me. 'The examiner has to *see* you do it, so make a bit of a song and dance about it. *Prove* you're following the correct procedure. Don't leave anything to chance.' It's just the same with a toddler. If they want you to look at the drawing they've just done, don't sneak a peak from behind your newspaper or chopping board and mumble, 'Very nice, dear.' Instead, stop what you're doing as a way to prove you're taking an active interest in what they want to show you. And if they want to tell you something, don't say, 'I'm listening, darling', and carry on with what you were doing. Give them your full attention by listening with your eyes as well as your ears.

No toddler tells their mum or dad something because they think it might be a useful piece of information to impart. They tell you things because they want the reassurance that comes from getting your attention. If you give it to them, it says, 'I love you.' If you don't, it suggests you have better things to do with your time than give it to them.

 Top Tip: *Toddlers spell 'love' T-I-M-E, so never skimp on the amount you give them.*

A Stitch in Time

The fact is, the clock is ticking and time is running out. Your child's toddler years will be over and gone before you know it. In fact, their whole childhood will be over a lot sooner than you think. Before long they'll have grown up and left home. As difficult as it is to grasp right now, in the grand scheme of things there aren't many summer holidays, Bonfire nights, Easter bunny hunts, Pancake Days, conker collecting sessions and Christmas Eves when your child will want to be with you. So the task of every wise parent is to grasp every opportunity they have during these fleeting toddler and childhood years firmly, and with both hands. Seize the day, because it'll soon be over.

IT'S TIME MUM AND DAD
REALISED THE BEST GIFT
THEY CAN GIVE US IS TIME...

You may feel that you can't really afford the time right now to meet all your toddler's demands. In the light of all the other calls made on your time and energy, reading to them each night or taking them to play on the swings in the park at the weekend may not seem to come very high on your list of priorities. But time passes very quickly and before you know it the boot will be on the other foot. One day, in the not too distant future, *you'll* be the one phoning to ask if they're too busy to pop home for the weekend. Rather than you finding time for them, they'll be trying (you hope!) to fit *you* into their hectic schedule and busy social diary.

Most of us order our priorities on the assumption that we'll be around for many years to come. We put off doing *important* things because we're frankly too busy trying to do all the *urgent* things that keep piling up. We work all hours in order to get a promotion at work and tell ourselves there'll be more time to spend with our children later on. But for a toddler, 'later on' is usually 'too late'. They need our love and undivided attention *now* if they're eventually to develop into sensible, mature and self-confident adults.

As the saying goes, 'A stitch in time saves nine'. If you fail to invest time in your toddler now, you run the risk of storing up more trouble for yourself later. It's a bit like investing in a new company: unless enough money is put into it at the outset, it'll never be able to do more than survive, limping from one crisis to another in a permanent and chronic state of under-investment. By contrast, if there's a healthy injection of cash upfront, there's a very good chance the company will do well. So invest heavily in your toddler's life *now* – you'll never regret it.

Top Tip: *Your toddler will be grown up before you know it, so take the opportunity to invest in their lives **now**!*

'If Only ...'

When a senior and rather stern lawyer, with a reputation for working very long hours, was asked what she'd do differently if she had her years to live over again, she replied, 'I'd eat more ice cream and laugh more. I'd ride more rollercoasters, sing louder in the bath, stay up late more often watching films with my friends, and spend a *lot* more time with my children!'

It may be a cliché, but it's still true: no one ever said on their deathbed, 'I wish I'd spent more time at the office.' So why do so many of us – men and women – act as if the office were more important than our family? And why do the rest of us so often allow the housework to tire us out, or get between us and our toddler?

Most of us like to think we're pretty important at work. So much so, in fact, that we risk getting mesmerised by our own sense of self-importance, and end up losing our grip on reality. Don't fool yourself: however crucial you think you are in your job, someone else will eventually take your place. It's painful to admit it, but you're *not* indispensable. Except, that is, at home, where there's no replacement for you – you're unique. So from the moment your toddler is born, your main 'job' is being a parent.

It's easy to blame your job or the housework for the lack of time you have to spend with your toddler. I know that when Emily and Daniel were small, I was convinced it was the 'unique' pressures of my job that made it so hard for me to find the time to spend with them. But as I've grown older and hopefully a bit wiser – and the kind of work I do has changed – I've slowly come to appreciate the uncomfortable truth that it's my *personality*, not my *profession*, that makes it hard for me to find the time.

It's a fatal mistake for someone in paid employment to behave as though 'work' stops the moment they leave the site or finish sifting through papers. In fact, we need to work every bit as hard at home as we do in our workplace. But don't despair, because investing quality and quantity time in your toddler isn't just the *right* thing to do, it's also highly rewarding and great fun!

Of course, it's never easy finding time for your toddler. But then, it isn't easy finding the time to mix a passion for work with a passion for football, squash, aerobics, golf or even the pub, club or gym – yet busy working men and women have been managing for years. As they say, 'Where there's a will, there's a way'. It's a myth that the right moment will come along, or something will happen, so that you suddenly have more time to spend with your toddler. The fact is, you *can* spend more time with them if you want to, and if you're disciplined enough to make the appropriate choices.

Top Tip: *You're a parent **first** and a worker **second**, so try to give each responsibility the time it deserves – no more, no less!*

'To Work or Not To Work ...'

Sometimes these choices are dramatic. Cornelia and I made the conscious – and costly – decision when Emily was born that only one of us would go out to work. It's meant only one salary coming in, which has always been a struggle and has sometimes been a source of depression and anxiety. We've been unable to afford some of the things many of our friends have taken for granted, for themselves *or* their children. There were times when we seriously wondered if we'd made the *right* decision. But looking back now, with the power of hindsight, we both feel it was a price worth paying. In fact, faced with the same choice, we'd do the same thing again.

Fifty years ago, mothers were expected to stay at home and raise their children full time. Working mums were rare and house-husbands unheard of. Recent changes in work practice, however, have meant that more and more mothers are in paid employment, either because they *want* to be or because they *have* to be in order to make ends meet financially. This can create a lot of guilt – not just in mums who go out to work, but also in some who opt to stay at home but somehow feel they *should* be out working and earning.

In an ideal world, every child would have a mum and dad who lived together in a loving, committed, permanent relationship, where one earned enough to ensure that the other had the option to be a stay-at-home parent, and they *both* invested a lot of time in their child. In reality, however, our world is far from ideal. Through divorce, desertion, death or design, a great many children live with only one parent, who normally has to go to work. And even with two parents, there's often still a financial need for both to work.

Though studies have shown that toddlers are neither emotion-ally nor academically scarred by being cared for by someone other than their mum or dad during the day – so long as the quality of care is high – this doesn't stop most working mums feeling guilty. To some extent, I think, the reason for this guilt is that women are still brought up to feel they *should* be at home looking after the kids. But even more importantly, the majority of mothers – unlike the majority of fathers – actually *want* to look after their children either full or part-time. It's the 'maternal instinct'.

Frances, a successful business executive, had a four-year-old child and was pregnant for a second time. Her husband was equally busy and successful, and they relied on a live-in childminder to take care of little William. They always made sure one of them was there to give him his breakfast in the morning and read him a story at night, no matter how busy they both were, and made every effort to see as much of him as they could. Nevertheless, Frances couldn't shake her feelings of guilt at being a working mum. In the end, the strain of being what she called an 'absent mother' and trying to juggle work and motherhood became overwhelming. She had a miscarriage on a business trip, which she blamed on stress. The tragic loss of her baby, she later told me, made her 'come to her senses', and she resigned her job to spend more time at home.

Growing numbers of working mums opt for a part-time arrangement, combining a career – albeit no longer on the fast track – with a greater degree of stay-at-home motherhood. From traditional part-time work to job sharing, freelancing or 'telecommuting' (working from home using a phone, fax machine or e-mail to stay hooked up to the office), there's an ever increasing variety of options available, and employers are often keen to explore these rather than lose a trained, valued member of staff.

Not all fathers, of course, are immune to the idea of being a full-time parent, and there's no reason at all why they shouldn't be *the* full-time parent. Some dads actively want to do it, while for others it's the natural choice because their income or career potential is less than their wife or partner's. And just like some working mums, some dads combine looking after a toddler with working part-time, freelance or from home.

If you do go out to work full-time, especially if you're a single parent, day-care and childminding facilities are essential. Look for ones ideally that are close to where you either live or work, and where the staff have a healthy dollop of common sense and take a genuine (rather than purely financial) interest in caring for your toddler properly during the hours when you can't. But above all, don't imagine that they can ever replace the time *you* need to spend with your toddler. It's no good fetching them from nursery school or a registered childminder and assuming they've received their 'recommended daily dose' of human contact. In fact, rather than reducing a parent's need to spend time with their toddler, leaving them in the capable hands of child-care professionals actually makes finding this time even more important. After all, you're still their mum or dad. There's no replacement for you.

Top Tip: *Child care can't replace you, so if you **do** go out to work, make sure you still give your toddler the time they need.*

'A Time for Everything ...'

Balancing family with work and other interests and responsibilities is a constant struggle, and just when you think you've got it sorted, something else comes along to throw a spanner in the works. It's a bit like walking a tightrope. It's not a case of struggling initially to get your balance and then, having done so, finding that you're free to carry on regardless afterwards. Staying upright on the high wire is a *continuous* process of making tiny, but absolutely vital, adjustments.

A good way to begin getting the right balance is to take a large piece of paper and write down everything you do during the average day or week, and roughly how long it takes: from child-care activities to leisure, and from work to sleep. Then take another piece of paper and draw a large 24-hour clock (or seven clocks if your week is irregular). Starting with what you *have* to do, slowly try to fit all your daily activities into slots on the clock.

The chances are, you'll find it's an impossible task. Like trying to fit 'a quart into a pint pot', it just won't go. If that's the case, you'll have to make some uncomfortable choices. Some things will have to be given less time in order to make time for others, while some things will have to go completely for now. (Though it wasn't actually true, it often felt as though the only 'hobby' I had left when our kids were toddlers was sleeping!)

But be careful: don't try to make too many changes too soon. Many good intentions fall flat because the goals people set are over-ambitious. So learn to walk before you try to run. The more realistic and sensible your goals are, the more chance you have of fulfilling them. For example, if you're spending too long at work, don't try to get home two hours earlier every day. Instead, have a go at thirty minutes twice a week, so you can read your child a story before they go to bed. If you have a partner who also works, see if they can do the days you can't, so you share the load. The secret is to start small, but make it a priority.

> **Top Tip:** Make time to spend with your toddler – and start **today**!

A Breath of Fresh Air

When you travel on a plane, a member of the cabin staff always carefully explains what to do in case of a 'loss of cabin pressure'. 'An oxygen mask will drop down automatically from a compartment above your head: place it over your head, fasten the straps, and breathe normally.' But there's an extra little instruction for parents: fasten your own mask *before* trying to fasten your child's mask. The reason they have to be so emphatic about this point is because, as we all know, most parents would naturally help out their child before taking care of themselves. But in fact, trying to fit an oxygen mask over the head of a frightened, perhaps even panic-stricken, child is difficult and often time-consuming. If a parent is struggling for breath at the same time as trying to fit their child's mask, the result is likely to be disastrous for both of them.

This 'oxygen-mask principle' also extends to the rest of a

parent's life. So as you draw up your 24-hour clock, don't forget to put in time for yourself, and time with your partner if you have one. The mistake some parents make is to spend virtually every waking moment either working or caring for their child, without creating or protecting a little 'oasis' of time for themselves. As a result, they're almost permanently exhausted, and never really feel on top of things. The irony is, this isn't an efficient way of coping. In fact, it isn't really a way of coping at all.

When Henry arrived in Stuttgart to start his new job, he was a bit intimidated by the 'efficiency' of the German workforce. He was dismayed to find that his colleagues arrived for work at 8.30 a.m. and didn't leave until about 8.30 p.m., often taking extra work home with them. The office environment was such that anyone who did less than a twelve-hour day was considered lazy and in-efficient. With a young family to look after, Henry was determined not to follow their example. Instead, he left work at six, making sure he was back in time to tuck his two young children into bed before spending the rest of the evening with his wife. This early de-parture was frowned on by his colleagues – until they realised that he *wasn't* lagging behind in terms of his workload. Though he worked ten hours a week less than they did, he seemed to be *more* productive. The reason? He was better motivated and more able to concentrate because he was getting more rest.

Rest and 'sanity time' are vital parts of a parent's day. Some-times this means relaxing with a bottle of wine after the 'human tornado' has gone to bed and you've cleared up their mess. At other times it means plonking them down in front of the TV to watch the *Teletubbies* or a *Postman Pat* video, just to give you half an hour in the middle of the day to regroup and recover your energy. Once a month or so it may mean getting your own mum or dad, or someone else you and your toddler both trust, to baby-sit while you get a night out at a restaurant or the cinema, or perhaps even a whole day at a friend's or in the country. Sometimes finding 'sanity time' will mean taking up a specific hobby, or even part-time work, so your brain (and body) are exercised doing something constructive that has nothing whatsoever to do with your toddler.

The important thing is, as they say, to 'work smarter, not harder'. Block in time for yourself, your work, your toddler and your partner (if you have one), but make sure that you're being realistic in the amount of time you dedicate to each. Don't try to make too drastic a change at once, and don't be put off by the number of times you fail to reach your objective or by the length of time it'll take to get your new lifestyle – because that's what it *is* – up and running. At the same time, recognise the importance of being with your toddler as much as you can during the 'formative years' of their life. It's a serious investment to make, but one that'll pay huge dividends for both you and them later on in their life.

Top Tip: Don't forget to create 'sanity time' for yourself in the diary: you'll **need** it if you're going to stay on top of things.

'But Of Course I Do'

How Can I Show My Toddler I Love Them?

It's funny how easy it can be to give people the wrong impression. You may be crystal clear in your own mind what you're trying to say, but other people can still get the wrong end of the stick with surprising ease. The consequences can be murder – sometimes literally! When King Henry II uttered his famous cry, 'Who will rid me of this turbulent priest?', he was just blowing off a bit of steam. He was upset with the Archbishop of Canterbury, Thomas Becket, and couldn't help exploding. But a small group of his knights – being better equipped in the brawn than the brains department – took his words literally and, sword in hand, murdered the Archbishop at the altar of his own cathedral.

If it's that easy for adults to get the wrong end of the stick, just think how much easier it must be for toddlers. After all, they've got none of the powers of deduction or benefits of experience that their elders have spent years slowly acquiring. In other words, if you're not clear, careful and consistent in the signals you send your toddler, they may misunderstand what you're trying to say. Things that seem blindingly obvious to you may be very far from obvious to them. Good communication with your toddler isn't about what you think you've said – it's about what they've understood.

From the moment I held my first child in my arms, I knew I'd *always* love her, no matter what she did or failed to do in her life. I didn't love her because of the warmth of her personality or what she had to offer – we didn't really know each other, and the only things she had to offer me were what looked like radioactive nappies and sleepless nights! Instead, I loved her because I loved her, and for no other reason. But I slowly became aware that just because *I* knew this, it didn't automatically follow that *she* did. Toddlers aren't mind-readers, so parents need to be explicit in letting them know they love them unconditionally, because they won't necessarily be able to deduce it for themselves.

 Top Tip: *Toddlers aren't mind-readers, so let them know you love them (with no strings attached) in everything you do and say.*

Your Love Is King

Loving their children unconditionally isn't hard for most parents – it comes naturally. In 99 per cent of cases, there's an instant biological bond of love between mums and their kids. Even dads, who haven't carried the child for nine months, feel an irresistible magnetism. And this feeling isn't one-sided. All children grow up instinctively loving and trusting their parents. They want and need their attention and acceptance.

While in the womb, your baby receives all the nourishment they need through an umbilical cord. This cord is cut at birth, but your child remains attached to you by a kind of invisible, emotional 'umbilical cord' throughout their toddler years. They rely on you to provide them with all the love, support and affirmation they need not just to survive, but to thrive in life. If they learn from you that they're a unique and valuable person, they're likely to be happy whatever life throws at them. If they don't, they may well spend their whole life searching for the love and acceptance they didn't feel you gave them.

One of my favourite films is *Forrest Gump*. Forrest is an intellectually subnormal child who's also physically disabled, and can only walk straight with the help of leg braces. This marks him out as an obvious target for school bullies. But thanks to his mother's constant love and reassurance, he grows up with the strength and courage he needs to handle all the put-downs life throws at him. More than that, he manages to be both successful and, more importantly, extremely happy. By contrast, his only childhood friend, Jenny – whose drunken father regularly abused and beat her – spends most of her adult life in a desperate search for the love she never had as a child. Despite being beautiful, brainy and charming, she's crippled by her inability to believe that anyone could love her for who she really is.

If your toddler develops the kind of security and self-esteem that come from knowing you love them with no strings attached, you'll have given them a massive head-start in life. But if they don't, they'll always be at a big disadvantage. As their mum or dad, you have by far the biggest influence on them during their formative years. The impression you give them about what they're like as a person will shape their character for many years to come. The more you let them know, through your words and actions, just how much you love them, the more likely they are to grow up happy, secure, self-confident and well adjusted – in short, able to get the most out of life.

This enormous responsibility is not one a wise parent can risk leaving to chance. But tragically, and without meaning to, we often end up sending our children the wrong signals. For instance, when their innocent clamouring for attention annoys us after a hard day, or when we tell them off for being naughty, if we're not careful they may interpret our behaviour to mean that we only love them when they're quiet and perfectly behaved – which, of course, is totally impossible for a toddler! So be *proactive* in reinforcing the message that you love them unconditionally, rather than just taking it for granted that they somehow *know* anyway.

Top Tip: *Your toddler* **needs** *to know that you love them if they're to be happy in life, so don't leave it to chance:* **let** *them know.*

---

101 Ways To Say, 'I Love You'

The first and simplest way to let your toddler know that you love them is to tell them. Not only is it amazing what a difference those three little words can make, it's just as amazing how hard some of us find it to say them. If we're not used to it, it can be embarrassing to be so open and honest about our feelings. Men, especially, seem to find it enormously hard to tell their partners, and often their children, that they love them. I'm constantly surprised by how many teenagers and adults tell me that their dad has never told them that they love them. Somehow they just never get round to it because it's a habit they've never acquired. But it's a message that toddlers – and children of all ages, for that matter – desperately need to hear, and a habit well worth forming.

And even if we regularly tell our kids we love them with no strings attached, it's no good at all if everything else we say and do sends them a different message. It's vital to reinforce our words with lots of practical evidence.

A few years ago, there was a television advert for diamonds that featured a variety of different ways husbands could tell their wives, 'I love you.' One man hired a billboard with the slogan, 'I love you, Mrs Jones' (presumably his wife!). Another spelt out a similar message using an impressive firework display, while a third trailed a banner behind a plane. Set against these 'fleeting' demonstrations was a man giving his wife an expensive-looking diamond ring. 'A diamond is for ever,' said the caption. But the truth is that, though the diamond may be for ever, there's absolutely no guarantee that the love it's supposed to demonstrate will last that long. Without the vital oxygen that making time for each other provides, any relationship will suffocate. Besides, love isn't something you can buy. Our *presents* are always empty and meaningless if they're not accompanied by our *presence*.

Instead, practical evidence means three things: attention, conversation and contact.

Attention. 'You can't live on bread alone,' as Jesus famously said. Food and water aren't the only things growing children require. They need huge amounts of attention. For a toddler, attention is as essential as oxygen – without it, they die.

This is no exaggeration. A few years ago, I was invited to visit a government children's home in Thailand. State resources were stretched to the limit, with the result that there were considerably more orphans than there were places for them or staff to cope. As a result, many orphaned toddlers were simply left alone to vegetate. Starved of the love and attention they desperately needed, with no one to stimulate their minds or personalities, they became effectively mentally disabled, not developing properly either intellectually or emotionally.

None of us, especially toddlers, can survive without attention. It's a vital component for our mental and emotional well-being. If you don't give your child the attention they need, they'll come to the obvious conclusion (to them) that they don't deserve it, and all your efforts to build their self-esteem and assure them you love them unconditionally will be undone. By contrast, if you *do* give them the attention they need, they'll not only develop properly, they'll also realise just how much you love them.

A few months ago, a friend wrote to tell me his dad had died. 'How can I describe him to you?' he wrote. 'He was a mixture of the softest compassion and a hardness forged by years fighting in some of the toughest wars ever. His tenderness with his children was amazing, raising four boys on his own after his wife died, being both mother and father to us. He was frantically busy, but he always found time to come to my football matches and school events.' By making his sons a priority, he showed them just how important they were to him. Looking back, my friend added, 'He was an extraordinary man. I'm so glad he was my father.'

Conversation. Sometimes attention just means being in the same room as your toddler and occasionally watching them as they play. Your presence tells them you're happy just to be around them, and you like having them there. But at other times they need you to take a more active – and verbal – interest in what they're doing.

Unlike adult conversation, conversing with a toddler often means that one of you does the talking and the other does the listening. Toddlers are often much better at asking questions than they are at listening to the answers, especially when it comes to the question, Why? They can ask it over and over again, even when they

45

know the answer. The reason for this is simple: as well as satisfying their curiosity, getting mum or dad to answer questions is a way of getting their attention and feeling secure.

Never forget that the pleasure of the conversation – whether a toddler is talking or listening – is usually far more important than its content. We shouldn't be surprised at this, of course: adults do exactly the same thing all the time. We don't often turn up for an evening with friends, over a meal or a drink, complete with an agenda of 'topics for urgent discussion'. What matters isn't what we talk about – which is often forgotten by the next morning – but the enjoyment we get out of spending time talking with each other. The truth is that talking is simply a means to that end.

Sometimes, of course, the tables are turned and all your toddler actually wants you to do is listen. Unless they're a budding Einstein, what they actually say probably won't be earth-shattering – but that doesn't mean that *listening* to them is unimportant. My friend Rob remembers the time his four-year-old daughter, having tried in vain to get his attention for almost an hour, climbed on to a chair, looked him straight in the eyes and yelled, 'Is there anybody in there?' Listening to your toddler is a way of telling them that they're *worth* listening to, which automatically tells them that you care.

Contact. Never underestimate the importance of touch. Physical contact is a vital way of expressing love – from cradling a baby or hugging a child to shaking hands with a friend or making love with a partner. Touch is important whatever a person's age, but a toddler finds particular comfort and reassurance in a parent's hug, or holding their hand. It may seem awkward, and sometimes even embarrassing, but touch is an essential part of telling a toddler, 'I love you.'

Top Tip: *Let your toddler know just how much you love them by giving them the attention they deserve.*

Regular as Clockwork

Toddlers tend to be much more secure and happy when they live in an organised, structured environment. The world is a big and scary place when you're just two or three years old, and you rely very heavily on your mum or dad to keep you safe and sound. For this reason, it's vital for a toddler to have the kind of familiar home atmosphere where they feel safe, secure and in control.

We often like to think of ourselves as being spontaneous and unpredictable, but the truth is that we're all very largely creatures of habit. From the time we wake up and go to bed to the activity of our hormones, we tend to be governed by regularity and routine. It's part of the rhythm of nature, and the effect of tampering with it too much – as anyone who's ever suffered from jetlag will tell you – can be very disruptive. Routine is important to all of us, but it's especially important to a toddler, so it's vital for you to give them as clear, consistent and predictable a pattern of life as you can.

For example, they should know when it's time to get up or go to bed. They need to have regular slots for breakfast, lunch and dinner. They should be able to know roughly when to expect a bath, a story, a walk, a snack, a snooze or playgroup. This kind of daily routine will help them build the confidence they'll need to cope with their surroundings. Anything out of the ordinary can seem bewildering, if not frightening, to a toddler. By contrast, a predictable routine builds familiarity, and familiarity in this instance breeds *content*.

VERY IMPRESSIVE, MUM... BUT IT'S NOT QUITE THE ROUTINE I HAD IN MIND...

Top Tip: *Toddlers thrive on routine and structure, so try to create a clear, consistent and predictable daily pattern for them.*

An Anchor in the Storm

Of course, consistency isn't only important when it comes to set-ting your toddler's daily routine – it's just as vital when it comes to *your* behaviour. If you're not consistent in the way you treat your toddler, and in how they see you behave, they'll struggle to make sense of life. Toddlers aren't immune from stress: they desperately need to know they can rely on you to take care of them, as well as where they stand with you.

Familiarity is extremely important for toddlers. Their under-standing of the world isn't yet well developed, and they tend to be easily scared and wrong-footed. For example, from the ages of about seven to eighteen months (though it can persist to the age of four years or beyond), many toddlers are virtually inseparable from their mum. They're never far from her, and can feel really anxious if they become separated from her. Being near mum is a crucial source of comfort in a confusing world. In a secondary way, tod-dlers also tend to find comfort from blankets, teddies, dummies, dolls or thumbs. It doesn't matter what it is; what matters is that it's *familiar*. It's dependable. It provides a much-needed anchor in the storm of life.

As their mum or dad, of course, *you* are your toddler's ultimate anchor. The more predictable your behaviour is, the more secure they'll feel – the more unpredictable it becomes, the more frighten-ing and bewildering everything will seem to them. Your toddler isn't really able to understand the concept of a 'bad day' – even if they have one themselves now and then – so they're unlikely to be too sympathetic or make allowances for you when you've had a tough time and your head's pounding like the drum section of a brass band. If you snap at them, or let your mood or ill temper influence the way you treat them, you'll only make them confused and frightened.

The more consistent you are in the way you treat them, the more familiar they'll become with you, and the more confident they'll be in their surroundings. As odd as it seems, your consistency tells them you love them. It tells them you can be relied on – that you'll always be there for them.

 Top Tip: *You're the anchor in the storm of your toddler's life, so try to make sure you're consistent in the way you treat them.*

On the Rocks

Families come in all shapes and sizes, and many of them, for one reason or another, have only one parent. However, if you have a partner, the quality of your relationship with them will have a huge impact on your toddler. Constant rows, or even just the slow grinding down of a negatively charged atmosphere between mum and dad is bound to create an air of tension and insecurity around the house. Of course, toddlers won't understand this tension – and certainly not the reasons for it – but, in spite of that, they're absolutely guaranteed to be affected by it.

Toddlers aren't old enough to have developed a sense of other people's needs and wants. They see everything simply in terms of how it affects them – *now*! If your relationship has hit a rocky patch, it'll inevitably ratchet up the tension levels in the house. As your toddler notices the change – and they undoubtedly *will* – they'll become more tense and nervous themselves. If your relationship is unpredictable and uncertain, they're bound to feel a little unsteady and less secure. As a result, they won't feel as confident, and in extreme cases may even take a few steps backward in terms of talking, toddling or, if they're a little bit older, bed-wetting.

You may also find that they misbehave a lot more. This isn't just because they're following your example and learning new skills in bickering. It's that, if you're busy rowing with each other, you're almost certainly giving *them* less of your undivided attention. Most toddlers learn fast how to grab their parents' attention, and if they can't get it for good behaviour, they'll take it in any shape or form it comes. Even negative attention is better than none at all. In short, they'll resort to whatever it takes to get your attention back, and if throwing a tantrum or misbehaving will do the trick – fine!

Secure families produce secure children, so it's vital that through all the loo-cleaning, nappy-changing, vomit-clearing, kid-ferrying, clothes-washing, key-losing, meal-cooking, sink-unblocking, supermarket-shopping, cat-feeding, bill-paying, mundane tasks of everyday life, you work hard to keep the romance alive in your relationship. It's important to find times – and appropriate baby-sitters – for the two of you to go out together and to enjoy yourselves. It's not pampering: it's survival!

Don't be afraid to kiss or cuddle one another in front of your toddler. Knowing that you love each other helps reassure them that you love them, too. (After all, if you can fall out of love with each other, what's to stop you falling out of love with *them*? That most mums and dads who go through a break-up couldn't stop loving their toddler if they tried isn't at all obvious to the toddler!) And when the romance isn't there, keep working hard at loving each other through all the arguments and hard times.

If you're struggling in your relationship, it may be a good idea to get help from a professional counselling organisation like Relate (see the list of organisations at the end of this book). They'll be able to help you think and talk through your problems – either on your own or with your partner. Whatever you do, don't just give up or try to sweep things under the carpet in the hope they'll disappear. Take action and deal with them *now*! It's too important not to – for you *and* your toddler!

> **Top Tip:** *If you have a partner, your relationship with them is the heart of your family – if it's a constant war zone, it'll have a detrimental effect on your toddler.*

Crunch Point

But what if things have reached the point where you and your partner are thinking about separation or divorce? Is it better to stay together for your toddler's sake or not?

For the last thirty years, most child-care experts thought that staying together was always counter-productive. Children were robust enough, they argued, to accept that you couldn't stay together. What mattered to them most was that you were both happy and free, instead of feeling trapped. But recent research has turned this view on its head. The days of pretending that kids don't mind whether their parents decide to split up or not are over. The fact is that all children, whatever their age, function better in a secure and settled environment. They learn better, behave better and develop better. Unless there's ongoing domestic violence, they're happier when their loyalties aren't being divided. So the view now is: if at all possible, *do* stay together for the sake of the children.

Sometimes, of course, staying together isn't an option. You've sought help and done everything you can think of but it makes no difference. Your relationship simply won't work. Sometimes you don't have a choice. Your partner has walked out and you're on your own. And on top of all your other worries, you're very concerned about how your toddler is coping. So if you do separate, get divorced or find yourself abandoned, what can you do to help them adjust better to their new situation?

- Constantly reassure them they had nothing to do with the break-up of your relationship. It's not their fault that you can't get on with your former partner. This may be obvious to you, but it's far from obvious to them. Don't wait for it to become an issue. Tell them as clearly and simply as you can, together if possible, as much as you think they can understand – which isn't much if they're one year old, but considerably more if they're four.

- Separation is like bereavement, so whatever you say, be prepared for your toddler to go through periods of denial, resentment, anger, confusion and grief before slowly coming to terms with the situation. They'll need lots of attention and reassurance, so expect their behaviour to get worse!
- Tell them about all the practical problems, and answer all their questions as honestly as you can. They'll want to know where they are going to live and how much they'll see of each of you. They'll feel very insecure and worried about big changes.

Above all, don't use your toddler as a pawn in your own power game. You're divorcing each other, not them, so don't use them as a weapon or try to get to your ex-partner through them. They need the love and support of *both* of you, so never moan about each other in their presence. Whatever you may think of your ex-partner and their behaviour, don't run them down in front of your toddler. Children automatically love and respect both of their parents. If they hear you badmouthing your ex-partner, it won't help their respect for you either.

 Top Tip: If at all possible, **do** stay together for the sake of your toddler.

'If You Don't Stop Crying, I'll Give You Something to Cry About!'

How Do I Discipline My Toddler?

Life wasn't easy for the codebreakers of Bletchley Park, Britain's top secret World War II 'listening post'. Their task was to monitor all the encoded German radio signals, work day and night to crack their codes and then supply that vital information to the Allied forces. Getting the code right was nothing less than a matter of life and death.

For the average toddler, struggling to understand the baffling world into which they've just been introduced is rather like trying to crack an extremely complex code. Things only begin to slot into place bit by bit. All of us rely on having a clear 'code of conduct' which tells us how we fit into everything around us – for instance, how we're meant to behave and relate to others. And though we all ignore it from time to time, we still depend on it being there to help us not only make sense of life, but also to make a positive contribution to it.

One of the key tasks facing every parent is to instil in their toddler this 'code of conduct', because the moral 'code' they learn from you now won't just help them make sense of their life as a toddler – once they've mastered it, it'll stay with them through the years and guide the choices they make as an adult.

The process of teaching children a moral code is usually referred to as *discipline*. The problem is, discipline has a rather bad press. For many of us, it's a word that conjures up Victorian images of children being 'seen but not heard'. A century ago, parents were stern, table manners were impeccable and punishment was severe. 'Spare the rod, spoil the child' was the household motto. Discipline was all about punishment, and punishment was all about the cane, the belt or – if your mum and dad were the soft type – just the slipper!

In fact, the word 'discipline' comes from a Latin word which simply means 'instruction' or 'system of knowledge'. And it's still used that way in universities around the world: an 'academic discipline' – such as history or physics – is a particular branch of knowledge. So the truth is that disciplining your child doesn't mean *torturing them to make them behave*; it means *training them in how to behave*. Discipline is all about giving them a moral framework – a code of conduct – for their life. It's there to help them make sense of their life, and achieve the most with it.

That's why it's so important for your moral 'code' and your style of discipline to be consistent. It's hard enough for a toddler to work out what the code is in the first place, but if you keep changing it – letting them do something one day and punishing them for doing it the next – they're bound to end up confused and even scared. And because they won't have been able to 'crack the code', they'll be at a huge disadvantage when it comes to knowing what to expect and how to behave around other people. So not only will they be an increasing handful at home, they'll also be a real menace whenever you have to take them somewhere else. However you look at it, good discipline is the result of consistency.

 Top Tip: Discipline isn't about punishment – it's about giving your toddler a consistent code of conduct for life.

Cracking the Code

Toddlers are bursting with energy. They're little human dynamos, primed and ready to go. But because they're so incredibly energetic, it's easy for us parents to make the big mistake of assuming that it's their massive energy levels that make them such hard work. In fact, that's not the case. The truth is that toddlers *don't* have too much energy – they have too little guidance! They're like *un*guided missiles. They desperately need a way to channel their energy constructively. Discipline is really just a means of helping them do this.

It used to be felt that there was only one way to tame a horse and make it ridable: break it. In the last ten years, however, a new method has emerged known as 'horse whispering'. The idea is simple: to harness the horse's energy *without* breaking its spirit. Its defenders claim that it's not only a lot quicker, but it also produces a better and more willing horse than breaking ever can. A parent has the same basic aim: to harness their toddler's energy and enthusiasm *without* breaking their spirit. And any discipline worthy of the name needs to have this as its goal.

The problem is that parental 'discipline' can all too easily degenerate into little more than a chance to work off our own anger or frustration on our toddler. At the end of a long and exhausting day, it's so easy to view a toddler's actions as 'the last straw'. Whether they're making a noise, making a mess, asking questions or wanting help, it all just seems like too much to cope with. So they find themselves being shouted at, banished, threatened or even smacked for tiny violations of the code – or worse still, for no reason but our unpredictable mood swings. It's not their fault: they're just the unfortunate and vulnerable 'victim' who happens to be in the wrong place at the wrong time.

The truth is, of course, that – all other arguments aside for a moment – aggressive, angry or uncontrolled lashing out doesn't actually work as a form of discipline. It's confusing rather than clear and consistent, so it doesn't help the toddler learn how to 'crack the code'. In the end, all they really learn is how unfair their mum or dad is. What's more, this kind of 'undisciplined discipline' isn't just ineffective. It's *counter-productive*. Rather than building up a toddler's sense of confidence and self-worth, it breaks them down. Ultimately it's bound to undermine and corrode a parent's relationship with their toddler, which means that undisciplined discipline isn't just a recipe for failure. It's a recipe for absolute disaster.

Top Tip: *Toddlers don't have too much energy – they have too little guidance. Discipline gives them that guidance system.*

'All You Need Is Love'

Because of the horrors of excessive punishment and undisciplined discipline, some parents now feel that *any* kind of discipline is outdated and dangerous. 'A healthy family life', it's said, 'is about letting kids have what they want and do what they want. It's about giving them the freedom to express themselves.' But there are two big problems with this idea. The first is that, as a mum or dad, you have to *live* with this 'freedom of expression'. Toddler taming is hard at the best of times, but living with a 'free range' two-year-old is enough to tax and destroy the patience of even the greatest saint. To put it very bluntly, left to their own devices every toddler is a 'home wrecker'. So if you want to keep your sanity, you'll need to keep a lid on your toddler's behaviour.

The second problem with giving free reign to your toddler's self-expression, choosing not to discipline them, is that it creates *undisciplined* children. I recently talked to parents whose son was totally out of control. His behaviour was no longer just embarrassing: it was now dangerous, both to himself and others. 'I can't understand it,' they said. 'We gave him everything he wanted.'

Unfortunately, that was precisely the *problem*! If a child is given everything they ask for, they come to learn they can have anything they want. And the older they get, the more problems this will create. The solution to *ab*use isn't *non*-use but *correct* use. Abuse of discipline ('undisciplined discipline') is a terrible thing. But absence of discipline leads to an equal and opposite tragedy.

Good discipline ultimately produces *self*-discipline. And however painful it seems at the time, both to you and your toddler, it tells them you love them far too much to let them be destructive and self-destructive. It says, in effect, 'I love you too much to let you flush your life down the toilet!' So the challenge for all parents is quite simply to *dare to discipline*.

 Top Tip: *Good discipline lets your child know you love them, and gives them the building blocks for developing self-discipline later in life.*

The Famous Five

A tiny minority of toddlers seem to emerge from the womb with a full working knowledge of how to behave at Buckingham Palace. These little angels eat whatever is put in front of them, sleep when they're meant to and cause their parents no trouble at all. If your toddler is like this, consider yourself lucky. Most of us end up with toddlers who spent their time in the womb not learning how to become angels, but right little terrorists.

Of course, *toddler* terrorists don't behave antisocially out of a sense of malice. In fact, there are only five basic reasons why your toddler might be acting up. Understanding these, and making the correct diagnosis, will help you considerably in knowing how to respond to them, giving them the security they need at the same time as reinforcing your code of conduct.

1 Tiredness. All of us get whingey when we're tired. We lose our ability to concentrate, and our temper gets shorter than normal. Toddlers are exactly the same. When they're tired they cry more, complain more, resist more and make far more mistakes. If you suspect the problem in your toddler's behaviour is tiredness, a few early nights and midday naps will do them and you the power of good. Review their naptimes and bedtimes, and make some adjustments if necessary.

Toddlers need lots of sleep, but they rarely get all they need during the night. As a result, they usually need to top up their batteries for an hour or so, once or twice during the day. By the time they're about two, they should survive on a single 'siesta', which they can often dispense with altogether by the time they're about three. The golden rule is to ensure their waking times, naptimes and bedtimes are as regular and routine as possible. The more you alter this routine, the more tired and whingey they'll become.

2 Frustration. Your toddler is growing and developing every day. As part of that process, they're constantly discovering new things they can do – and just as many they can't! Every new achievement is a cause for celebration, but every failure is a giant source of frustration. Think about the sheer number of skills your toddler is struggling to master, and ask yourself whether the reason they're acting up is actually because they're frustrated by all the things they can't yet do, or perhaps by the changes their body is going through (e.g. teething).

3 Ignorance. I'll never stop being amazed by the senseless things toddlers do. I remember when our elder son, Daniel, was two, Corni made some curtains for his room. They looked brilliant in the window – for all of about a week. Then we noticed that one of them seemed to have shrunk a bit. When we examined it more closely, we realised it had been hacked off with Corni's menacing-looking pair of fabric shears! Both the shears and the offcut were lying on the floor directly under the curtain, so it didn't take Sherlock Holmes to work out what had happened. Our suspicion fell on Daniel – who calmly denied all knowledge but, budding chemist that he was, offered the theory that the bottom had 'probably fallen off' due to an inherent weakness in the fabric. We weren't convinced. He couldn't think why.

A lot of the senseless things toddlers do aren't done out of deliberate mischievousness, but simply because almost all toddlers – especially younger ones – have a near complete and utter lack of common sense. To a toddler, the 'long-term future' is at most sixty seconds from now, so imagining the consequences of any action beyond that is virtually impossible. This can lead to some dangerous situations. I still panic every time I see a swing because of the amazing lack of sense and self-preservation Abigail showed when she was a toddler. Oblivious to Emily's attempts to be the first child in the history of lawn furniture to loop the loop on a garden swing, she'd run out right into the 'flight path', risking – and often getting – a boot in the jaw. Most amazing of all, however, was the fact that, no matter how many times she got hit, she never quite made the connection.

These situations aren't 'disciplinary' matters in the sense of needing punishment. Though a single, light smack on the hand might do a lot to reinforce a parent's cry of 'no' where the outcome could potentially be dangerous, the main thing is to find a way to curb your toddler's natural instincts as they gradually evolve some common sense.

4 Attention. One of the most common reasons for a toddler acting up is their constant need for attention. It's just as vital to their proper development as food, sleep and exercise. If your toddler feels they're not getting enough attention, they'll let you know – just as they let you know when they're hungry. In fact, if they're hungry enough, people will eat the most extraordinary things – things they wouldn't dream of eating in normal circumstances. It's the same with attention. If your toddler can't get 'premium' attention – the kind they most want and need – they'll settle for whatever form they *can* get from you. Even anger is better than nothing. In other words, if they can't command your attention by being well-behaved, they'll *mis*behave. If they're naughty enough, you *have* to stop what you're doing and pay attention to them, even if it's only to tell them off! But although you may need to punish them for misbehaving, by far the most effective way to 'cure' this kind of acting up is to find them things to do to stop the boredom, and give them the attention they need.

5 Challenge. In Steven Spielberg's blockbuster dinosaur movie, *Jurassic Park*, the hi-tech theme park's staff have the daunting task of keeping real genetically engineered dinosaurs – particularly the deadly velociraptors – well out of harm's way in specially constructed high-security holding pens. However, when they're first put in their cage, the raptors constantly attack the electrified fence, but never in the same place twice. As one of the staff explains: 'They were testing the fences for weaknesses, systematically. They remember.'

In the same way, your toddler will constantly test both the boundaries you set down and the way you enforce them, looking for weaknesses. But unlike the raptors, your toddler will take huge comfort from the fact that the fences are firmly in place and can't be breached. The truth is, for all their complaints, they need to know you're keeping a close eye on their conduct. They need to know you're in charge and you're looking out for them. It tells them you care. So it's vital for you to respond clearly and decisively to any challenge your toddler makes. If you don't, you'll be storing up trouble for yourself – and them – later on.

Top Tip: *Understanding **why** your toddler is misbehaving will help you know how to respond in a way that'll reinforce your 'code of conduct'.*

The Secret Seven

When I was young, I used to enjoy a good game of chess with my father. Unfortunately, they never lasted long. I was sure he was just a step away from becoming a Grand Master, because he always used to beat me in a few easy moves. Whatever gambit I tried, he never failed to land me in checkmate within minutes. Back then, I was baffled. Now I realise that the secret of his success was that he'd studied my 'technique' closely enough to see how utterly predictable my moves always were.

Your toddler may *appear* to have an endless repertoire of dastardly tricks up their sleeve, but if you could take a step back from all the confusion and chaos for a moment you'd see that all their moves are actually just variations on a few simple themes. That's good news, because it means that once you've learnt to recognise a few tell-tale signs, there's a very strong chance that you'll learn to predict their actions and plan your response accordingly.

There's no Universal Handbook for disciplining your toddler. For one thing, disciplinary theory is as subject to the tides of fashion as hemlines and haircuts. When I got married in 1980, though I say so myself, I looked really cool. But things change, and when I look at our wedding photos now, I'm astonished by my choice of hairstyle and clothes. In exactly the same way – and almost as quickly, it would seem – parenting 'fashions' change. When Emily was born, for example, she was swiftly taken away to a cot in a different section of the ward to ensure that Corni had a 'vital opportunity to rest and recuperate'. By the time Joshua was born six years later, however, things had changed and Corni was encouraged to spend time 'bonding' with him only a few minutes after the birth.

But there's another reason why a Universal Handbook would be useless. Every toddler is different, so what works with one child might not work with another. If you don't take the time to get to know your toddler inside out, you'll never know how to discipline them in a way that's appropriate to their personality. What's more, you'll never develop the kind of strong relationship that'll enable you to be *effective* in disciplining them. The greatest secret of good discipline isn't to do with the techniques you use on your child, but the strength of the relationship you have with them. In the end, it won't make much difference how often you send them to their bedroom or smack them if your relationship has deteriorated to the point where you don't have any real authority over them any more. If they don't know you love them, then whatever techniques you try to use, you'll be fighting a losing battle.

In the context of a loving relationship, however, there are seven main tools in a parent's toolkit for effectively disciplining and bringing order to their toddler's life: *prevention, diversion, swiftness, ignorance, assertiveness, smacking and praise*. Virtually every form of effective discipline falls into one or other of these categories, but which you use will depend both on your circumstances – including an idea of *why* your toddler is acting up – and on their temperament.

Top Tip: *There are seven main ways to discipline your toddler, but how effective they are will depend on the strength of your relationship.*

1 Prevention: How To Toddler-proof Your House

Whoever first said 'prevention is better than cure' must have experienced living with a toddler. For our family, visiting Corni's mum always used to be a rather tense and nervous experience. It wasn't that we didn't enjoy going – quite the opposite. It's just that her house was packed with expensive and extremely breakable objects, most of which were carefully positioned at toddler height. Every time we went round there, it was a real struggle to keep a check on the kids' natural inquisitiveness, and ensure that no more than one or two valuables got chipped or broken on any one trip!

The easiest way to make sure that none of the valuables in your *own* house go missing or get mysteriously broken is – don't keep them anywhere a toddler can find them. Invest in some high shelves and lockable cupboards for the safekeeping of anything that won't survive being mauled by grubby fingers, inserted into tiny mouths, knocked or dropped. And don't take them out until everyone in your household is over the age of four!

This, of course, applies equally to things like bleach, detergent, cleaning agents, polish, medicines or anything else that could possibly poison your toddler. Most families *without* toddlers choose low cupboards, such as those under the sink, to store these things. Once your child becomes mobile, however, it's best to play safe and keep harmless food stuffs in the lower cupboards and anything potentially dangerous well out of reach, preferably with a lock or catch on the door. Some good friends of ours discovered the wisdom of this first hand one day when their son, Tom, stood on a stool, climbed up to the bathroom cabinet, took his dad's razor from inside and proceeded for some completely unfathomable reason to shave off his eyebrows! He looked silly for a week or two, but his mum and dad learnt not to underestimate a toddler's climbing skills, and always to keep potential hazards under lock and key!

It's not just small things that are breakable, of course. When we first got married, we couldn't afford to buy a video recorder, so we hired a prehistoric, second-hand one from a shop – a decision we'd later come to celebrate. To a toddler, you see, the slot for the video cassette on the front of the machine looks just like a letter box – perfect if you want to send your piece of toast and marmite to a friend! I've lost count of the number of times we had to call a repair man out, but I remember thinking how fortunate we were that we'd hired from a shop that included unlimited free maintenance in the contract. Only when Joshua turned six did we actually dare to *buy* our own machine.

It's impossible to toddler-proof your house completely, of course, but there's still a lot you can do to prevent your toddler doing senseless things that drive you up the wall. You don't need to scour the house on all fours inspecting everything from a toddler's-eye view, but it's definitely worth noticing what you've left within reach of your mobile monster, and working out how much harm it could do them – or they could do to it! After all, you can't really blame your toddler for adding thin horizontal stripes to your wallpaper at the one-foot-high mark if you left them unattended and the crayons out!

WHAT'S THE MOST TODDLER-PROOF PART OF YOUR HOME?

THE PARTS THE TODDLER ISN'T ACTUALLY IN.

Top Tip: Prevention is better than cure, so work hard at toddler-proofing your home.

2 Diversion: 'And Now for Something Completely Different'

One couple I know have solved the problem of living in a 'non-toddler-friendly' house by having a sofa full of teddy bears in their sitting room for whenever their toddler nephews and nieces come to visit. Learning from the wreckage left after the first few visits, they found that having a 'toddler magnet' in the lounge meant that all they had to do afterwards – unless it was a long visit – was count to see if any teddies had mysteriously vanished!

Creating a diversion is a time-honoured way to deal with toddlers. Often the root of their 'misbehaviour' is boredom or lack of attention, so giving them something to concentrate on can be a very effective way of calming them down. A toddler's attention span is short, so they'll forget about being upset or unhappy very quickly if they're given something fun, exciting and engaging to occupy their mind. If you're visiting a friend with your toddler in tow, make sure you pack a few of their favourite toys in your bag – something that'll keep them busy without much risk of them inflicting damage on your friend's house (leave the finger paints at home!). Of course, no toy is an alternative to your attention – your toddler will still need the reassurance that comes from your active attention every few minutes.

Diversion is also an extremely effective way of defusing a tense situation at home. Adults do it by 'changing the subject' of conversation, but when it comes to a toddler, you'll need to find some way of giving them something else to do – reading a book together, playing a game or even watching a video – as soon as you suspect that a tantrum is coming along. Or you could try changing the mood with a bit of humour: a silly voice, a funny face, a song etc. If they're acting up in the car, play one of their favourite tapes or CDs and get them to join in with the music or story.

Sometimes, of course, it's not your toddler that's about to throw a tantrum. It's you. If they've slowly driven you up the wall all day,

or you've come back after a very tough day at work to find that they won't stop yelling and screaming, and have surgically attached themselves to the bottom of your leg, then you'll probably find yourself having to use all your powers of self-restraint just to stop yourself from exploding.

The 'time out' technique – taking them to their room and leaving them there for a few minutes to play by themselves – can be very effective as a diversionary tactic, giving your toddler something new to do and giving you a few moments of peace and quiet in which to calm down and cool off. It's a distraction: pure and simple. After five minutes or so they'll resurface, in need of some more personal attention, but by then your anger or frustration should have blown over. If they resurface too quickly, after less than a minute, take them back to their room, shut (*never* lock) the door and go back to what you were doing. Don't linger and don't worry about them: if you've toddler-proofed their room, they're safe.

71

Top Tip: *Giving your toddler something to do can diffuse a situation fast.*

3 Swiftness: Getting the Habit

On 28 June 1914, Archduke Franz Ferdinand, heir to the throne of the Austro-Hungarian Empire, was assassinated outside Sarajevo town hall. It was a fairly minor event as political assassinations go, yet within six weeks the whole of Europe was embroiled in a colossal war that would claim over ten million young lives. Why? To put it simply, because the so-called Great Powers of Europe embarked on a game of bluff and counter-bluff, convinced that sooner or later one of them would back down. At its most basic level, World War I broke out because a handful of powerful nations let a small dispute escalate out of all proportion.

In a very similar way, all too many parents court trouble by allowing minor problems to develop and get completely out of hand. I recently travelled to France on business, staying with a family where three generations live under the same roof. As I sat in the kitchen, trying not to get in the way of supper being prepared, I watched Dominique, the family's two-year-old daughter. Perched on her grandmother's lap, she was showing great interest in a bowl of water that was on the table. At first she dipped one finger into the water, very gently, giggling. A few moments later, she dipped another finger in. After a few minutes of this, the novelty started to wear off, so she put her entire hand into the bowl before drawing it out again and instinctively shaking it, flicking a small arc of water across the table. Very excited by this unexpected outcome, she put her hand in the bowl again and began flicking water over the table and everyone in range! Rather than stopping her, Dominique's granny seemed amused by this game, which was gradually drenching the rest of the audience. Then suddenly, after another few minutes of happy flicking, Dominique picked up the bowl and poured the rest of its contents all over her grandmother, who rather rapidly – but somewhat belatedly – ceased to see the funny side of things!

It's often hard for a parent to tell the difference between innocent experimentation and 'misbehaving'. For example, when your one-year-old throws food onto the floor from his spoon, is this a scientific experiment into the effects of gravity on a viscous object released from a high chair, a stubborn refusal to play along with the 'mealtime' game, or a failure to have mastered the relevant motor skills? Parents who want to be fair face a big dilemma: do they tell their toddler off for misbehaving, or assume they're too young to know any better and let them continue dropping food on the floor?

The truth is, it doesn't really matter. Toddlers acquire habits even before they're aware of what they're doing, which means that the longer parents tolerate 'performance art' on the floor, the harder it'll be to change such behaviour later on. So whether it's exploration, mischief or lack of co-ordination, quietly and calmly helping their toddler guide the spoon to their mouth will get the job done with the minimum of fuss. And if at all possible, my tip is to avoid having to pretend it's a plane or a train, with accompanying sound effects. This may work well in the short term, but in the long term it'll only transform every mealtime into a theatrical event, with the toddler demanding ever more elaborate performances from their parents.

> **Top Tip:** Don't wait for a problem to become a crisis before acting – look for the 'early warning signs' and be decisive.

4 Ignorance: How To Become Selectively Deaf, Dumb and Blind

If your toddler is bored and wants attention, but you're busy doing something else, you can almost guarantee they'll start misbehaving. As I've said, if they can't get your 'premium' attention, they'll settle for whatever form they *can* get, including your frustration or even anger. They'll do whatever they can to provoke a reaction from you. But if you *do* react, you've lost. They'll have got your undivided attention, which is what they were after, and having learnt to do it successfully, they won't hesitate to use the same technique again and again in the future.

On a recent trip to a supermarket, I saw this demonstrated in two very different ways. In both cases, the toddlers involved were misbehaving because they were bored – both mums were busy filling their trolleys with the week's shopping, leaving their respective

offspring with little to do but follow idly around. Each began playing up. The first mum's response was to try to keep her toddler in line by swearing at him and whacking him. But the words and wallops were clearly having little effect on the boy because, while not quite immune to the pain, he'd learnt to settle for his mum's anger and slaps as a step up from boredom. In the next aisle, the second mum's two-year-old daughter was having a great time knocking baked bean cans onto the floor. 'Please, Charlotte darling, stop that,' her mum pleaded, as calmly as she could. But the more she begged little Charlotte to stop, pointing out the error of her ways as sensitively as possible, the more Charlotte happily knocked cans off the shelf, eventually graduating from the baked beans to the tinned tomatoes, and from there to the sweetcorn!

The problem was that both mums were unwittingly rising to their toddler's bait. If your toddler is bored, they'll do whatever it takes to get your attention, and misbehaving is one of the easiest ways of achieving that goal. What's more, if it works, they'll keep doing it.

So what should those mums have done? Some parents long for

the day that Tesco's or Sainsbury's introduce trolleys with not just child seats, but sound-proof and child-proof safety cages (complete with non-stop *Teletubbies* videos) built in. In the meantime, however, there are four basic ways to make shopping a bit less like hell:

- Avoid the problem altogether by leaving your toddler at home in the capable hands of a partner, parent or baby-sitter – my preferred option.
- Have a go at 'supermarket sweep', seeing how fast you can get through your shopping list. The goal here is to finish before your toddler's attention span has wandered too much, so they never have time to get bored.
- Turn the whole thing into a big adventure, involving your toddler as much as possible in choosing the food and putting it in the trolley. This is the most energy-intensive option, and still something of a race against time to finish before they run out of enthusiasm, but you'll enjoy it a lot more than shouting at them.
- Ignore the misbehaviour altogether. At first this option sounds mad, impractical and dangerous – after all, isn't it the same as not disciplining your toddler at all? Of course, if they're making a rice mountain in the middle of the aisle, you'll need to take firm action. But if all they're really making is a scene, ignoring their misbehaviour can be extremely effective – provided you have nerves of steel and don't worry about what other shoppers may think. If your toddler is playing up because they want attention (rather than as a challenge), then even telling them off is a way of rewarding that misbehaviour.

Ignoring them shows that a tantrum is an ineffective way to get your attention. When they finally realise it isn't working – and you may need to use the same tactic in a variety of different situations for a few weeks – they'll give up. However, it's vital to realise that ignoring misbehaviour isn't enough on its own. You'll also have to get them interested and involved in what you're doing. That way you can alleviate their boredom without rewarding their naughtiness.

Top Tip: *Try not to reward bad behaviour by giving it too much attention.*

5 Assertiveness: The Tail That Wags the Dog

Jenny is watching TV in the lounge. Her son, Tim, plays with his toys on the floor by her feet. 'Time for bed,' she says sternly. But interestingly, neither of them moves a muscle for a good ten minutes. Then she repeats her command, louder and more sternly. Tim begins to sense that the dreaded moment is creeping up on him, so he says, 'OK – in a minute.' But again, neither of them moves. At the start of the next ad break, Jenny lays down the law: 'I really mean it, get up those stairs NOW!' Tim knows it's time to make some kind of token gesture, and slowly begins to pack up his toys. But he's been here before, and knows that whatever she says, she won't do anything until the end of the programme.

What does Tim learn from all this? That he can manipulate a

situation very effectively to get his own way. Jenny's first mistake was starting with an unreasonable command. If she'd given him fair warning that bedtime was in fifteen minutes, the element of surprise would have gone. He'd have had time to get used to the idea. And just as importantly, she'd have shown Tim that she respected what he was doing and didn't just want to spoil his fun.

But her fatal error was *not moving* when she told him to go upstairs to bed. This sent out conflicting signals: her words told him to go, but her body language said it wouldn't really matter if he didn't. According to experts, only about 10 per cent of our communication is verbal. The actual words we use have less impact than how we say them and what we do. Jenny wanted to see the end of the TV show more than she wanted Tim to go to bed, and this came out in her voice, her body language and her actions – or lack of them! If she'd looked him in the eye when she said it was time for bed, got up to go with him, and turned the television off, he'd have known that she meant what she said. Instead, she taught him to persevere until he got what he wanted, undermining her authority into the bargain.

It's amazing how many parents are scared to confront their toddler. Unfortunately, most toddlers are able to sense this fear and seem to have an instinctive ability to exploit it. So the tail gets to wag the dog! This is a recipe for disaster. If you can't control your three-year-old, you'll never cope with them when they're thirteen. The time to defuse the dreaded 'teenage time-bomb' is NOW! Good discipline takes lots of thought, courage, consistency, diligence, dedication and, of course, *time*. It involves knowing your toddler well enough to spot problems before they're allowed to become full-blown crises and confront your toddler in the knowledge that, as the parent, *you're* the boss.

Your family isn't a democracy – you have a legal and moral responsibility for your child. Not only do they not have the experience to call the shots, the truth is that they also need to know for their own peace of mind and security that you're in charge.

For instance, when you tidy up your three-year-old son's toys because it's time for bed, and he just tips them out over the floor again, what do you do? Do you say something like, 'Naughty boy,' and pick them all up again, just for him to repeat the process? Or do you lose your temper and make all sorts of threats which you don't mean and which, for all the noise, still don't teach him not to throw toys all over the floor? Screams and empty threats won't win you the day. In fact, yelling at your toddler is more likely

to under*mine* your authority than under*line* it – a quiet but firm command will be more effective than a frantic one. To win your toddler's respect, be firm and loving. Keep calm and exert your authority by putting your hands over his and gently making him put the toys back with you, before taking him up to bed. As much as anything, he's asking, 'Who's in charge?' And he needs a clear, self-assured answer in order to feel secure.

Top Tip: *Eye contact, movement and a quiet but firm voice let your toddler know you mean business when you tell them to do something.*

6 Smacking: Human Right Or Human Wrong?

Smacking is a big issue. An expert once explained on TV how smacking was a violation of human rights, likely to leave a child needing therapy. 'We've got to *talk* through the problems instead,' she concluded. Her interviewer was unconvinced: 'Perhaps a good smack is the right therapy sometimes,' she quipped. Who's right? Is smacking a form of punishment whose time is past? Does it scar children emotionally for life and teach them that violence is the way to solve their problems? Or can it have a positive effect, helping them develop the self-discipline they need?

Some people argue that smacking is wrong because, unlike other kinds of punishment, it's violent and abusive. But the truth is that shouting and screaming uncontrollably at a child can be every bit as abusive and emotionally scarring as an uncaring smack or slap. A few years ago, the director of one infamous children's home was sacked not just for beating the children in his care, but equally for using a system known as 'pin-down', where he confined them to their rooms for days at a time. The children considered this kind of 'solitary confinement' even more abusive than being beaten.

The problem, in other words, isn't confined to smacking. It goes far deeper than that. It's actually about the way in which *any* punishment is given. There's a world of difference between tapping a toddler lightly on the wrist and giving a ten-year-old an angry slap or a prolonged thrashing with a belt. In fact, lumping these together under one label – 'smacking' – as if they were all the same, is extremely misleading.

The truth is that *any* punishment given as an unthought-out, arbitrary or even violent reaction is abusive. Any punishment that's undisciplined and handed out in the heat of the moment is bound to be damaging. This kind of punishment will confuse and scar a child emotionally. And, just as importantly, it won't work.

But the double tragedy with out-of-control smacking is that the already devastating impact of emotional scarring and damage caused by undisciplined discipline is added to by physical pain and abuse.

 Top Tip: *Any punishment can be violent and abusive if given in an angry or unthought-out way.*

---

7 Praise: The Miracle Tool

Most behaviour is learnt. We avoid actions we know have bad consequences, and repeat actions that seem to be successful. A toddler won't hesitate to throw a tantrum in the middle of a crowded supermarket if they know from past experience that it'll get them what they want – a reward. In exactly the same way, Friday, our cat, always wakes me up first thing in the morning by meowing and scratching at our bedroom door. He knows I'll eventually get so sick of the noise that I'll get up, stagger across the bedroom, tiptoe downstairs to the back door and let him out. And though I hate to admit it, I know that every time I give in and do it, I reinforce his habit and make the chances of ever getting a lie-in even slimmer.

But exactly the same principle works for positive things, too. So if you want your toddler to go to the toilet by themselves, clean their teeth, pick up their clothes, tell the truth, be generous, be polite and courteous, or think of others, then praise is by far the most effective way to achieve it. Because if they like what happens when they do something, they'll do it again. Experts call this the Law of Reinforcement – 'behaviour that achieves desirable consequences will recur' – but to most of us it just seems like plain, old-fashioned common sense. So the golden rule is this: *Catch your toddler red-handed doing something right – and praise them for it!*

Praise your toddler frequently. But as you do so, make sure you're always:

- **Sincere:** Never let your desire to praise your toddler push you into lying to them. Insincere praise won't help. It's patronising, and will have the effect of completely devaluing any genuine praise you offer them on other occasions.

- **Specific:** Always be specific, so your toddler knows exactly what they did right, and gradually learns to recognise their strengths. Don't just say, 'That was good.' Explain why it was good.

- **Personal:** Praise your toddler for the effort they put into an achievement, not just for the achievement itself. If you praise them for what they've achieved, they'll start to link your approval and love with their success, not their effort.

- **Positive:** Don't follow your praise with advice on how to do even better. It'll send your toddler the message that *this* effort wasn't quite good enough. For example, if your son proudly shows you the Lego space ship it's taken him three hours to build, don't try to turn it into a finely engineered, fully functioning scale model of the USS *Enterprise*. It'll no longer be *his* creation.

- **Non-judgmental:** Toddlers develop in different ways and at different rates, so never compare their performance with someone else's. The only comparison that matters is with their own past performance. If they did *their* best, that's what counts.

Top Tip: Praise is the best motivator there is for good behaviour, so catch your toddler red-handed doing something right and praise them for it!

Last in the Class

What If My Toddler Is ... ?

Sally and her brother are stuck at home on a cold, wet day with nothing to do when the 'Cat in the Hat' bursts in through the front door. Determined to entertain them, the cat and his two accomplices, Thing One and Thing Two, cause mayhem. The two children are extremely worried. The whole house is a total mess – and their mother is due home at any minute. Even the fish starts shaking with fear at the prospect of her reaction to such chaos. So when the Cat in the Hat eventually starts cleaning up in double-quick time, everyone is relieved.

As soon as it was published, back in 1957, Dr Seuss' famous book, *The Cat in the Hat*, became an instant bestseller. Parents loved it as much as their children did because, for once, the roles were reversed: the mum in the story is happy and carefree, while Sally and her brother spend the whole time worrying themselves silly about the chaos the cat is causing. In real life, children don't tend to worry much about mess or anything else. Their parents, on the other hand, are usually consumed by all sorts of worry, especially during the toddler years.

When Emily, our first child, was a toddler, we worried about absolutely *everything*. Was she sleeping properly? Was she eating right? Was she developing fast enough, or too fast? Was she teething too soon, or not soon enough? Was she talking enough? Was she slow in learning to use a potty? Was her co-ordination good enough? Was she concentrating well enough? Was she too short? Or too fat? Were her legs bandy? Was her eyesight good? Was her hearing all right? Was she too shy? Or too selfish? What about her manners? We worried about everything it was remotely possible to worry about, and a lot else besides.

This worrying stage is entirely normal. I remember once hearing about a ninety-year-old woman who told a friend how relieved she was that she no longer had to worry about her children – she'd finally managed to get her youngest son into a nursing home! But although you never entirely stop worrying about your children, the amount you worry *does* diminish with time and experience.

This chapter tackles the *top ten trouble-spots* in toddler development, but before looking at them, it's important to make one thing clear. Corni and I worried because we thought we were *bad* parents. But the truth is, any parent who worries is a *good* parent. You worry because you're concerned about your toddler's development, and naturally keen to catch any potential problems early. You want the best for your child, taking your parental responsibilities seriously. By contrast, a bad parent won't care enough, and so won't notice enough, to worry in the first place.

 Top Tip: *Worrying about your toddler's progress is normal – you're not the only one doing it!*

1 Surgical Attachment

Our first three children seemed to cope quite well with our absences. If we were invited out for a meal, they'd be quite happy to stay at home with a baby-sitter. In fact, they often seemed so excited by the prospect of a baby-sitter's arrival that we wondered if they preferred it when we went out! However, our youngest, Joshua, was very different. He would frequently scream the house down if he thought we were even contemplating a night out. He'd cling to Cornelia and have to be peeled off before we could leave. As a result, we never really enjoyed going out, and always had to phone up halfway through just to check that both Joshua and the baby-sitter were all right! On more than one occasion we had to abandon the evening altogether and return early after an emergency call from home!

Separation anxiety is very common in toddlers. It usually begins at around the age of nine months – about the time they become aware that you're not actually a part of them and that you're not entirely at their beck and call. Children of this age tend to bond mainly with the parent who cares for them most – usually the mother. They become genuinely and sometimes inconsolably anxious during any period of separation, unable fully to grasp the idea that their mum or dad will be back. Though it tends to reach a peak at about fifteen or eighteen months, separation anxiety can continue until the age of three or four, or beyond.

Every toddler will sometimes cry for a while when their parents leave them in the hands of a grandparent or baby-sitter, but not every toddler suffers from full-blown separation anxiety. If they *do*, rather than crying for five or ten minutes and then finding amusement or distraction in something else, they'll rarely if ever settle down. They'll often continue to scream, cry and sob until their parent returns.

If your toddler suffers from separation anxiety, here are five more tips to help you cope:

- Be sensitive to their feelings. As with any phobia, your toddler needs reassurance, not reproach. They need to know you love them, you're not abandoning them to the child-catcher in *Chitty Chitty Bang Bang*, and – most importantly – you'll be back soon.
- Ensure that there's a decent 'hand-over period' between the time the baby-sitter arrives and the time you have to leave. Getting them comfortable with their carer is important, which is why, if at all possible, a relative or someone else they know well is a good option at this age.

- When you do leave, don't hurry out, but make sure you exit decisively rather than constantly changing your mind.

- As well as leaving a contact number where you can be reached if necessary, it's a good idea to phone the baby-sitter after an hour or so to see how they're doing and whether or not you ought to return. Talking to your *toddler* on the phone probably won't help, but since they're already anxious it can't do much harm either. (By the way: there's no real evidence that separation anxiety does any permanent psychological damage to a toddler – though it might just drive the sitter up the wall!)

- If the anxiety persists, it may be an idea to go out for shorter periods – arrange to drop round to friends just for a coffee rather than a whole meal – so that you can gradually build up your toddler's tolerance for separation. The root of their fear is not realising you'll be back, so just going out for a short time may slowly help prepare them for longer periods of separation in the future.

 Top Tip: *Separation anxiety is very common in early toddlers, but in the long term it's far more traumatic for the baby-sitter than for your child!*

---

2 'These Boots Were Made for Walking'

A typical toddler starts to 'toddle' at about thirteen months, though the age range varies between about seven and eighteen months. Before this, your little 'bundle of fun' is only mobile on all fours and could more accurately be described as a 'crawler' than a toddler. If you're worried about the slowness with which your toddler seems to be developing their walking skills, or concerned that they're a bit shy and ponderous in their crawling, then ask your GP to do a full assessment of what's known as their 'gross motor' development. But bear in mind that there's absolutely no evidence that a toddler who takes their time before stepping out will be anything but normal in later life. Sooner doesn't usually mean better.

I'M WORRIED ABOUT MY TODDLER — HE'S NOT WALKING YET!

If you want to encourage your child to walk, the best way is to get personally involved. Encourage them to stand by using your hands as an anchor, and start them off walking short distances by holding their hands in yours and supporting some of their weight – anything that turns you into the toddler equivalent of a zimmer frame is probably good. The jury is still out on baby-walkers. Although they're no longer thought to produce bandy legs, some experts are concerned they might breed 'walker dependency', so a toddler could actually take longer learning to walk on their own as a result of using one. Whatever the merits of that particular argument, however, it's certainly true that walkers can create laziness in the parents. And if anything's going to help your child take their first steps, it's your attention and encouragement!

Don't expect your toddler to be too steady on their pegs for the first year or two. After all, they're a 'toddler', not a 'walker' – and even the *Oxford English Dictionary* is clear that to 'toddle' is to 'walk with short unsteady steps'. So expect them to fall over – a lot! And confine their toddling to soft, carpeted surfaces rather than on cold, granite floors as much as possible. In order to walk well, they need to develop their muscle control, improve their co-ordination, perfect their balance, focus their concentration and hone their visual depth perception. All this takes time and practice, so don't expect too much too soon, and make sure you boost their enthusiasm by giving them plenty of praise when they do well.

 Top Tip: *Sooner doesn't usually mean better – just because your toddler is biding their time before walking doesn't mean there's a problem.*

3 The Sound of Silence

'The French', someone once said, 'must be a very intelligent people – even their children can speak the language!' Learning a new language is always tough, but when it's your first, it's even harder. When our kids started learning French at school, they at least had a basic grasp of English to compare it with. But when a baby or a toddler starts to learn a language, they have to start completely from scratch. In fact, not only do they have to get a grip on the basic grammar and vocabulary, they also need to learn how to recognise and interpret the sounds they hear as intelligible words, as well as how to master their vocal chords in order to talk back. And all within the first few years of life.

Most babies start with the vowel sounds, because they're easier, and work from there to the basic consonants. By about six months old many are capable of combining both vowel and consonant into one-syllable noises like 'ba' or 'da', and by nine months they may have learnt to double this into 'baba' or 'dada'. But don't break open the bubbly just yet, because 'dada' to the average nine-month-old is more of a pleasant sound than an identifiable word. 'Real' words with real meanings don't generally arrive on the scene until about the first birthday, and even then the meanings are approximate. Our elder daughter Emily, for example, initially used to call *everything* a 'duck' – except ducks, that is!

Most two-year-olds have acquired a two-to-three-hundred-word vocabulary, which grows to a massive thousand words by the age of three and doubles again by the time they're four. Like walking, however, rates of speech development vary enormously. Emily had an impressive vocabulary by the time she was one, and was able to string short sentences together. Our first son Daniel, on the other hand, was so reluctant to talk that until he was about four we thought he'd taken a vow of silence and would end up becoming a Trappist monk! He's since made up for it, of course, and it's now impossible to tell that he and Emily were at opposite ends of the spectrum when they were learning to talk.

The best way to encourage your child to go vocal is to talk to them. Eye contact, gestures and constant repetition are the order of the day. Talking is about a lot more than words – *how* we say things communicates just as much as *what* we say, so make sure your toddler gets a chance to study your tone of voice and facial expressions, not just your vocabulary. Use simple words, and say them clearly, enthusiastically and often. This is the recipe for success used by mums and dads through the ages, as well as TV stars like Tinky Winky, Laa Laa, Dipsey and Po from *Teletubbies* and, for older toddlers, programmes like *Sesame Street*. Above all, praise them whenever they get it right – or *almost* right. If they say 'boog' rather than 'book' praise them *as if* they'd got it exactly right and then repeat the word clearly and correctly ('that's right, "boo*k*"!').

Talking, of course, is a mixed blessing. Once your toddler has started, there may be no stopping them, and you're bound to get frustrated by their constant wittering and repetition. But bear with it – they need the practice as much as they need *your* input.

 Top Tip: *Don't worry if your toddler is slow to start talking – they'll probably make up for it later!*

---

4 Mr Sandman ...

- Are you woken in the night by your toddler's incessant crying?
- Do you come to in the morning feeling like a zombie, only to find yourself half off the bed with your toddler's foot in your back and your partner exiled to the downstairs sofa?
- Do you wake engulfed by a warm feeling because your child has climbed in with you and wet themselves again?

Yes? Well join the club!

Sleep problems are very common with toddlers. Though some appear able to sleep right through the night, the majority will often wake up in the middle. In fact, toddlers – just like adults – go through sleep cycles, waking up or almost waking up about every sixty minutes (ninety for adults). This is entirely natural, and it only becomes a problem if the reason for their waking is something like teething, illness, bed-wetting or a nightmare – in which case they'll need to be comforted – or if it disturbs the parents' sleep (after all, sleep deprivation is an ancient and extremely effective form of torture!). In other words, unless your toddler is in genuine distress, their midnight waking is only a problem if it's a problem for *you*.

Sleep is an essential requirement – and the less disturbed it is, the better. So one of your aims has to be to get a good night's sleep yourself. Being a toddler, or the parent of a toddler, is hard enough when you're firing on all cylinders, but when neither of you is getting your full complement of sleep, the tension levels in the house are bound to rise, which is bad news for everyone.

Listening to your toddler cry for long periods is hard – very hard. After all, crying is one of the great success stories of evolution – it works! If they cry, they get your attention. It's a 'conditioned response'. If it *didn't* work, toddlers would eventually stop doing it – which, of course, is the whole point, and the secret to achieving more uninterrupted nights' sleep. The reality is that, the more you reward your toddler's midnight cries with attention, the more likely they'll be to cry again. So the rule is, use minimal intervention. If they're in distress (and you'll *know* when that's the case), then of course you should see to them within a couple of minutes. But if they're just whimpering, put up with as much as you possibly can before you act. The tougher you are, the longer this will be. Try gradually lengthening the interval of time between your visits – from five or ten minutes to fifteen or twenty. And when you do see to them, make sure the experience is as 'grey' as you can make it: if you turn it into an exciting event, you're bound to be up and down all night for weeks! Eventually you should be able to go through the whole night, most nights, with no disturbances.

Here are four more tips you might find helpful:

- If they keep getting up when you put them to bed at night, take them straight back, comfort them, tuck them in and leave.
- If they specialise in making a fuss or inventing requests at bedtime, be gentle but firm. Try to build a consistent routine, and never spring their bedtime on them: giving them fair warning is likely to make them far more compliant. Most toddlers need about twelve hours' sleep, though some can survive with less. So when it comes to setting bedtimes, work out what time you want

them to wake up – or what time they habitually wake up, especially if they're an early riser – and count back from there.

- If they wake in the night having wet the bed, give them less to drink in the evening. What goes in, must come out!

- If they come into your bed after a nightmare (about a third of all three- and four-year-olds suffer from regular nightmares as their imagination starts to kick in), take them back to their own bed immediately and comfort them there. The more you let them invade your bed, the more they will – and believe me, you'll live to regret it!

JUST FOR A SECOND I DREAMT
I WAS GETTING A FEW SECONDS
OF UNINTERRUPTED SLEEP...

Top Tip: *Uninterrupted sleep is better for both your toddler and you, so don't reward their midnight crying with attention unless something is wrong.*

5 Growing Pains

Take a good look round you next time you're in a crowd. Everyone you see is different: different heights, different colours, different shapes, different hair, different styles and different accents. As they say, variety is the spice of life. If everyone were exactly like you, the world would be a much poorer place because of it. So why worry that your toddler may be different from everyone else's? Isn't that rather the point?

Toddlers are no more physically consistent than the rest of us, so comparisons with other toddlers are as fruitless as comparing ourselves with other adults – although, of course, this doesn't stop us from doing it! It's very common to see two children, roughly the same size, whose ages are actually months apart. As odd as it seems, there's no automatic connection between someone's size as a toddler and their eventual size as an adult. And though illness and diet can play a small part in determining your toddler's growth rate and final height, by far the biggest ingredient in this mix is their DNA. In other words, most toddlers grow to be the height and weight bracket their genes tell them to be, and *their* genes got instructions in the first place from *your* genes. So the chances are, if you're short, they'll be short, and if you're tall, they'll be tall. It's not an infallible rule, but it works most of the time.

Growth doesn't tend to be steady, however, and usually comes in spurts. Growth rates in the first eighteen months are faster than they are in the next eighteen months, so don't be surprised if your child's rapid development slows down during their time as a toddler.

Some parents worry that their toddler is either too fat or too thin, but just like height, the most important factor in determining your toddler's approximate weight bracket is their genes. Both adults and toddlers have a natural body 'type' – not everyone's born to be thin! – and going too much above or below the acceptable range for that 'type' won't be healthy. So provided you're feeding them a balanced diet, there shouldn't be any problem – toddlers take care of their own exercise programme!

Teething – which is virtually guaranteed to make your toddler more grumpy and irritable than usual, especially at night when tiredness makes them more vulnerable to pain and there are fewer distractions from the discomfort – is usually a two-stage process. Stage One, where six upper and six lower incisors break through the gums at the front of a toddler's mouth, usually starts at about six months, but it can begin as late as the first birthday. As terrible as it seems, however, this is just the warm-up act for Stage Two, when the mighty molars (four up, four down) begin surfacing some time between about thirteen and twenty months. Again, sooner doesn't mean better, and later needn't mean problems.

If you're worried about anything to do with your toddler's growth – from a recommended balanced diet to the advisability of using paracetamol to treat their teething pain – contact your GP or your pharmacist. If you're concerned about 'wasting' their time with 'minor worries', think of *yourself* as the real patient: it's your worry and potential worry-related illnesses, not your toddler's ailment, they'll be treating.

> **Top Tip:** *Nature takes its course and its time. The speed of physical growth varies dramatically from toddler to toddler.*

6 Food Fights

Carl and Olivia tried for years to have a child, and when little Nicola was finally born, they were so overjoyed they could never find it in their hearts to say 'no' to her. Starting with mealtimes, they spoilt her rotten. Literally. If she gave them trouble by refusing to eat her breakfast cereal, they offered her a choice of five others. If she resisted eating what they'd put in front of her for dinner, they rustled up something else. Everyone but them could see that Nicola had them wrapped around her little finger. She always got her own way. As a result, she's now a teenage tearaway and Carl and Olivia wonder what they did to deserve the abuse she seems to enjoy inflicting on them. But the answer is simple: they spoilt her.

The key ingredient in feeding your toddler is striking the right balance between *insistence* and *convenience*. On the one hand, you don't want to let your toddler dictate to you what they will or won't eat. If you're constantly running around after your toddler, getting them whatever they ask for rather than whatever you put in front of them, you'll not only spoil *them*, you'll exhaust *yourself* in the process. On the other hand, you don't want to turn mealtimes into war zones. If you're constantly fighting to get your toddler to eat whatever you put in front of them, you'll not only risk making mountains out of molehills, you'll also teach them that mealtimes are ordeals to be endured, not family events to be enjoyed. And once again, you'll exhaust yourself in the process. So if they refuse to eat what's put in front of them, you'll have to make a choice: either give them something you know they'll eat, or just take the food away and leave it at that.

My mum, like so many others of her generation, used to insist that I 'eat my greens', and never let me get down from table until I'd done so. But the truth is, this approach is usually more trouble than it's worth. If your toddler consistently refuses a particular type of food, save yourself a battle by not giving it to them. For example, if they hate peas but eat beans, or even baked beans, then don't cook them peas – give them beans instead! In time, their tastes will broaden and they may grow to like peas. However, if you turn the whole thing into a war, they may go off them for life!

If they refuse to eat a food you know they like, or won't finish their meal, it's usually not worth the effort to force them. Let them go without. *Your toddler won't starve if they miss a meal or two.* Like the rest of us, their self-preservation instinct will override their taste buds if need be. In the meantime, if they're tearing about the place, bursting with energy and never sitting still, they *must* be getting enough to eat – after all, they're burning a huge amount of 'fuel', so they must be getting it from somewhere.

If they complain later on that they're hungry, either offer them the food they turned down (assuming it's still edible) or give them a nutritious snack, such as fruit. Whatever you do, don't reward their earlier stubborn refusal to eat their meal by giving them crisps or chocolate now. And try not to give them too many unhealthy snacks between meals – the more crisps and sweets you give them during the day, the less room they'll have in their tummy for proper food at mealtimes. If you're worried that they don't seem to eat anything other than junk food, ask yourself who buys it for them in the first place – and make the decision to give them a more healthy, balanced diet in future!

Ideally, your toddler should be getting three regular meals a day, with one or two healthy snacks in between. Like adults, children need a diet drawn from three vital components:

- **Protein** (mostly found in eggs, meat or cheese);
- **Fat** (usually taken from meat, oils, nuts or dairy products);
- **Carbohydrate** (found in fruit, vegetables and starchy foods like cereals, bread or pasta).

Protein is essential for making hormones, enzymes and cell structures, while fat and carbohydrate are predominantly used as energy sources. Since toddlers generally burn up industrial amounts of energy running about the place, you're unlikely to need to worry much about your toddler's fat levels. (Contrary to popular belief, fat in the diet doesn't necessarily cause fat on the body – the key players on that score are calories. If you take in more calories than you use up, the body will store them as fat, regardless of whether they come from fats, proteins or carbohydrates.)

Try to give your toddler a healthy balance of all three – protein, fat and carbohydrate – as they contain the various different vitamins and minerals your toddler's body needs – as well as being, in some cases, a good source of fibre. In addition, your toddler needs plenty of fluid, the simplest and cheapest of which, of course, is tap water. If they're less than keen, however, try to stick with drinks that don't contain many added sugars or colourings. Milk or orange juice are the leading contenders, and won't rot their teeth like most fizzy drinks.

Try to introduce variety into their meals, experimenting with different tastes, textures and colours. But don't force it if they don't like it. Toddlers often have a limited repertoire when it comes to food, preferring familiar dishes and opting for bland or sweet flavours rather than complex or savoury ones. Subtlety is a trait few toddlers have learnt to appreciate, especially when it comes to their palate, so try to keep it simple but nutritious. If they're not sure about certain types of food, try to present them in an interesting or exciting way. For instance, one mother I know of used to give them bizarre names. When she couldn't get her son to eat his sandwiches, she simply renamed them 'gooey muck sandwiches', after which they became extremely popular!

> **Top Tip:** *Don't turn mealtimes into a war zone – force-feeding your toddler is usually more trouble than it's worth.*

7 What Goes In ...

When our youngest child, Joshua, was born, we had four kids (aged nought to six) and the most overworked washing machine in the history of the world! In fact, we used it so much that within five years it had completely given up the ghost and we were forced to replace it. The reason? Children, unfortunately, aren't born in control of the on/off tap for their bowel and bladder. It's a skill they only begin to learn when they're between eighteen months and two years old, and usually don't fully master for at least another couple of years after that. In fact, for the first eighteen months of life, most children are completely oblivious to the fact that what goes in must, or even *does*, come out! So here's the Chalke Family 'Track-Tested' Seven-Step Guide to Potty Training:

1   Your toddler is ready to be introduced to the potty as soon as they're able to sit up, even though this may be months before their muscles are developed enough for them to start controlling their on/off tap. It'll get them used to sitting on a potty before they're able to crawl off it again – after which it becomes much harder to get them to stay there!

2   Routine is vital. It's a good idea to make sitting on the potty an

after-meal ritual, since most toddlers soil their nappies after eating anyway, not through choice but as a reflex action. To make it more of an event, why not accompany it with a story? Toddlers rarely perform well under pressure, so the more relaxed you make it, the better. They need to see it as a natural part of life, not a test.

3 Don't expect miracles – they'll need time to get used to the idea. Most toddlers learn to pee a short while before they learn to poo, but the first milestone is simply getting them to sit comfortably on the potty. The rest will come later.

4 As with all toddler behaviour, you need to give praise when they've done well, to encourage them to repeat the triumph. If the idea of praising your toddler for going to the loo seems strange, you need to realise that what you're actually praising is the effort they're putting in to control their muscles – it's no less of an achievement than learning to walk, talk or pick things up.

5 Never chastise your toddler for failure. As with all 'motor skills', toilet skills take time to develop. Instead, downplay their mishaps and play up their achievements. Above all, don't let your frustration show if they won't sit still or if they soil their nappy just moments after an unproductive potty session.

6 Once your child is out of nappies, it's important to remember that immediacy is vital for toddlers, in bladder control as in everything else. If you're out and about and they tell you they need a pee, believe them. 'Holding it in' for long is totally beyond both their abilities and their concentration span, so look for somewhere fast. You've probably got about five minutes at the outside, so think resourceful not conventional! And try not

to tell them off for not having thought of it earlier: toddlers can't think that far ahead yet. It's better to encourage them to go anyway beforehand than blame them afterwards.

7   Your toddler may take time to learn *not* to wet the bed at night. In fact, 10 per cent of all five-year-olds still wet the bed, and it can sometimes continue up to age eight. It may be frustrating for you, but it's not a failing in them, so try not to get upset with them for it – tension will only make things worse. And never, *ever* tease them about it. Instead, praise them when they do it right.

 Top Tip: *Potty training usually takes place between the ages of two and three – praise their achievements and downplay their mishaps.*

8 Things That Go Bump in the Night

In Bill Watterson's cartoon strip, *Calvin & Hobbes*, troublesome toddler Calvin has a rather overactive imagination. This makes him permanently worried about the presence of drooling monsters under his bed at night. But his parents seem blind to the terrible danger he faces every time he goes to bed, and his only ally in his battle against such hideous evil is his loyal tiger companion Hobbes – a stuffed toy to everyone else, but a real hero to Calvin.

Every toddler has an active imagination – it's an essential requirement for everything from colouring to playing with dolls or teddy bears. The problem is that active imaginations don't always know when to turn themselves off. From nightmares to daytime phobias, a toddler can easily scare themselves without meaning to, just by letting their imagination roam unchecked. That's why a one-year-old is likely to be relatively fearless, but a two- or three-year-old will be much more prone to fear and distress. It's all simply the flip side of their developing imagination. To a toddler, the world can seem large and looming, full of the unknown and unfriendly. The problem is that, whereas every child needs imagination to help them make sense of the world, they don't yet have the kind of logical framework that lets them tell the difference between fact and fantasy.

However irrational your toddler's phobias might seem to you, they're extremely real to them. Joshua, our youngest, used to be scared of small enclosed spaces. He refused to go to the loo with the door closed and was petrified of lifts, screaming hysterically the whole time we were ever in one. So far as we know, we didn't do anything to give him this form of claustrophobia. He acquired it on his own.

Other very common fears include: strangers, sudden noises, pets, baths, the toilet, the dark, doctors, dentists, Santa Claus – just about anything! A good friend of mine once took his two-year-old son to see Father Christmas at a shopping centre. They had to pay £5 and queue for forty minutes, but when they finally got to the front of the queue and Santa greeted them with a booming 'Ho! Ho! Ho!', the boy was so scared he took one look and ran out of the grotto, screaming at the top of his voice!

There's no point telling your child off for their fears. They have no more control over theirs than you do over yours! And there's limited value in giving them rational explanations ('You can't be flushed down the toilet, Florence dear – the S-bend aperture just isn't wide enough to accommodate the circumference of your head'), since they don't think rationally. If you *do* give them explanations, keep them simple and remember that the reassuring tone of your voice will actually communicate far more than the flawless logic in your argument.

Above all, never belittle your toddler for being afraid of something, or tell them to 'grow up'. Instead, look for practical solutions. With Joshua, for example, we took the stairs whenever possible and held him tight if that wasn't an option. When it came to a fear of the dark, we found that keeping the relevant bedroom door open and a hallway light on solved the problem – though you could invest in a nightlight instead.

Attention is the real cure for this fear, however. But be careful: once your toddler has worked out they can get instant attention by complaining of being afraid, they may be crafty enough to prolong or even concoct a few phobias, so you'll need to wean them slowly but surely using exactly the same tactic as you would for separation anxiety (see above).

Top Tip: As an adult, it's your job to help your toddler cope with their fears, not expect them to cope on their own.

---

9 Bad Habits

Toddlers are an intensive breeding ground for bad habits. From biting and nose-picking to thumb-sucking, breath-holding, head-banging and interrupting, they develop all sorts of bad habits – both from their instincts and their surroundings (home, friends, playgroup etc.). Toddlers don't generally need to learn thumb-sucking or nose-picking from other people, for example. They just try it one day in their journey of self-exploration and find they like it. And when they later find out that you *don't*, that's an added benefit!

Some habits are acquired and lost quite quickly – especially if your toddler indulges in it to provoke a reaction and finds you're deliberately ignoring them. But if it continues, you'll eventually have to decide if it's worth the time and effort needed to eradicate it. Some habits, such as playing with their private parts, are just a harmless extension of their curiosity, and very common. Others, like thumb-sucking, can give genuine comfort and joy, and won't do any harm, whatever you've been told to the contrary.

With a dangerous habit, such as biting, you'll need to take a firm line, telling them 'no' and reinforcing this by either smacking them or doing something that deprives them of your attention – such as putting them in a corner of the room for a few minutes.

Top Tip: *Most toddler bad habits pass, so make sure a battle's worth fighting before you pitch in with all guns blazing.*

---

10 Never a Dull Moment

Lots has been written about Attention Deficit Hyperactivity Disorder (ADHD) – a condition formerly just known as 'hyperactivity' – yet medical experts still don't know precisely what it is or what causes it. Both ADHD and the related condition known as Attention Deficit Disorder (ADD) are characterised by an inability to concentrate or perform multiple tasks, but ADHD not surprisingly combines this with hyperactivity – in other words, seemingly inexhaustible levels of energy and activity. ADHD is a very hard condition to diagnose – especially in toddlers – because an ADHD toddler is exactly like a normal toddler ... only more so! And since doctors rarely like to diagnose any form of hyperactivity before the age of five, there's not much you can do even if your toddler *does* suffer from ADHD.

109

In recent years, some parents and child specialists have put their hope in a forty-year-old 'wonder drug' called Ritalin. Almost four million US children and adults are taking Ritalin in order to help them with their attention deficit problems, and the number of prescriptions is doubling every year in the UK. But while this amphetamine-like stimulant seems to be good at calming ADHD children down, there's no evidence that it does anything for them in the long run. In other words, if your toddler is hyperactive, there's no miracle cure yet.

So what can you do if you live (or should I say survive life) with a hyperactive toddler? The truth is that, since a hyperactive toddler is just like any other toddler – only more so – the way to cope is the same as with any other toddler – only more so. They need a routine, firm but loving discipline and lots of fun things to do. Toddlers aren't made to sit still and be quiet at the best of times. They're made to run around and explore, learning as much as they can in as short a time-frame as they can. That means that the most logical and sensible way of coping with them is to feed their minds and imaginations as well as their bodies. Boredom will quickly lead to demands for attention, and that's as likely to lead them into mischief as anything else.

The way to tame your hyperactive toddler is to try as hard as you can to keep up with them: give them things to do, encouragement to do them, and be patient when they lose interest or find it hard to concentrate. Praise them for their achievements, downplay their mishaps, constantly reassure them you love them, and make sure you find time by yourself to recharge your batteries.

Top Tip: *If your toddler is hyperactive, giving them things to do is likely to prove more successful than trying to calm them down.*

111

An Awfully Big Adventure

How Can I Make Learning Fun?

I recently went to a really 'traditional' wedding. The bride's parents, who weren't short of a bob or two, had spared no expense in order to give their daughter a day to remember for the rest of her life. The church was decked with flowers, the lavish reception was held in a beautiful historic building and the bride looked radiant in her fairy-tale white wedding dress. Even the two-year-old page boy looked perfect, almost like a miniature version of the groom in his top hat and tails.

But if his appearance was immaculate, his behaviour certainly wasn't. Rather than gliding serenely down the aisle behind the long bridal train, he sulked and slouched his way to the front of the church, propelled at regular intervals by one of the bridesmaids following behind. Once there, he refused to sit either quiet or still, and whatever she did, his mum couldn't seem to calm him down. He was clearly very unhappy in his starring role, and spent the whole service fidgeting, attempting to escape his mum's clutches and run up the aisle, and getting upset when she stopped him. I could tell from the chorus of tuts and disapproving looks that a large percentage of the congregation considered this behaviour totally unacceptable, and had decided to blame the mother for her son's antics. But I saw it all rather differently. Disruptive though it was, it wasn't the toddler's behaviour that was at fault. It was everyone else's unrealistic expectations.

We're often guilty of expecting too much from our toddlers. How often have you heard someone tell their child to 'act their age', when the problem was very clearly that they *were* acting their age? 'Boys will be boys', as the saying goes, but it's equally true that toddlers will be toddlers: expecting them to behave as though they were several years older is futile. Even if they manage to fulfil our expectations, there's no guarantee they'll be better off in the long run.

> **Top Tip:** *Toddlers will be toddlers, so try to make your expectations of them* **realistic**.

Dress Rehearsal

Some parents worry that, in such a competitive and often hostile world, their toddler will be hampered in later life if they don't get ahead early. As a result, they're keen for them to be able to read, write and do basic arithmetic before the age of four. To help them achieve this, they sometimes impose a regime of more work, less play. But while there's no doubt that this makes them look very impressive when they get to primary school, all the research suggests that these children are actually no better off than their peers academically at age ten or eleven. They may have had a head start, in other words, but that doesn't mean they'll necessarily finish first. Or at all, for that matter.

In fact, rather than being a recipe for success, this kind of 'cradle cramming' can prove to be nothing short of a recipe for total disaster. Instead of being *more* prepared for life in the real world, so-called 'superchildren' will actually be *less* prepared for it.

Has anyone ever told you that a job is so easy it's 'child's play'? We often forget what it's like to be a child. Playing is an all-absorbing, serious business. A child who isn't allowed to play enough is a child who doesn't adequately develop the skills they need to get on top of life. Play is both a way of learning to understand the world, and a much-needed rehearsal for the days to come.

The problem is that most of us have come to see learning as a narrow, formal thing. It means school, hard work and duty. Mark Twain once said that the definition of a 'classic' book was one that 'everybody wants to have read and nobody wants to read'. That about sums up our attitude to learning, as well. It's all about the 'Three Rs': reading, writing and arithmetic. It may be necessary, but it's deadly dull.

For a toddler, however, learning is a huge, exciting adventure and, alongside eating and sleeping, one of the three main occupations of life. For toddlers, learning is mostly about playing. Those who see play as nothing but frivolous entertainment make a big mistake. It's actually a multi-functional educational programme. In fact, there isn't a single part of your toddler's growth and development that won't be helped by them playing.

• **Physically,** play tones up their 'gross-motor' muscles (through running, jumping, lifting, walking, pushing, pulling etc.), as well as fine-tuning the dexterity in their 'fine-motor' muscles (in the hands and fingers). They'll gradually learn to manipulate objects, hone their hand–eye co-ordination, and perhaps eventually even … sit still!

- **Mentally,** play teaches them about colour, texture, taste, perspective, sound, smell, shape, sensitivity, cause and effect, light, dark, similarity, dissimilarity, mobility, immobility, right, wrong and, sometimes, even how to break things! In addition, it helps them to focus on things for increasingly long periods of time, slowly building up their concentration span to the point where they can perform more complex tasks.

- **Emotionally,** play lets them experience a range of different feelings, from frustration, anger and jealousy to love, joy and pride. By interacting with other adults or toddlers, and even by projecting emotions on to inanimate playthings such as teddy bears or dolls, they learn to handle their emotions in a safe environment, before too much is at stake.

- **Socially,** play gives them a chance to encounter, cope with and enjoy other people's preferences and personalities. It teaches them to talk, laugh and have fun with others, learning to respect their rights and property – and, of course, to share!

- **Personally,** play enables them to practise and master a variety of activities, which in turn helps to boost their self-esteem. It shows them some of their strengths and weaknesses, giving them courage to try their hand at things they've never done before. It also gives them a chance to learn how to handle failure, as well as how to strive for success again.

- **Linguistically,** play helps them learn how to express themselves simply, clearly and at a reasonable decibel level. Whether it's talking to people, pets, inanimate objects or even themselves, they get to experiment with word sounds, practising the vocal skills that will stand them in good stead in the coming years.
- **Artistically,** play gives them a chance to explore their creative side through acting, singing, dancing, drawing, painting, modelling or music, and helps them to develop their imaginations.

As well as learning these skills from scratch, however, play also gives your toddler the chance to rehearse them at length in a safe and comforting environment. The importance of rehearsal is obvious. Most of us get to practise things before we have to do them, especially if we have to do them in public. From driving or acting to exams or weddings, we benefit from the chance to rehearse. Few of us are able to get it right first time. A great dancer, for example, can make a performance *look* effortless, but a great deal of effort and discipline have actually gone into creating those few, faultless minutes. Fred Astaire used to rehearse his dance numbers so much and so carefully that it drove his fellow dancers up the wall, but the results delighted cinema audiences and gained him a reputation as one of the greatest dancers of the twentieth century.

Play, in other words, is far from messing around or wasting time. It's the basic way in which all children learn about themselves, their bodies, their environment and their place in the world during the first four or five years of their lives. The golden rule is: if your toddler can't learn it in play, they don't need to learn it yet.

Top Tip: *Play is serious business – it's the main way your toddler develops in every area of their life.*

Time for School?

Linking learning with school is actually quite recent. Before the 1800s, most children got little or no formal education, relying instead on their parents, apprenticeship or the 'school of hard knocks' to learn what they needed. But the nineteenth century saw a huge boom in primary schools, mostly funded and staffed by churches. The government stepped in to build schools of its own in 1870, and made primary school attendance compulsory in 1876. So *your* role in educating your toddler is in fact more time-honoured – and more important – than the school's.

By the time they're finally old enough to go to infant school,

117

probably just before their fifth birthday, you'll help both your child and their teachers if they can already:

- Recognise basic numbers and letters, though not necessarily words. Few children can actually 'sight read' *new* words until they're about six. Before then, the words they *can* read are ones they've slowly learnt to recognise only through constant repetition.
- Understand simple chunks of information or argument, processing them rather than just learning them parrot-fashion.
- Sit relatively still, listening to and following the teacher's instructions – especially when told *not* to do something.
- Move and manoeuvre objects with reasonable confidence and relatively good hand–eye co-ordination.
- Mix well with other children rather than behaving anti-socially by sticking to themselves or being selfish or disruptive.

Clearly, none of these things require your toddler to be Albert Einstein (who didn't show exceptional promise as a toddler anyway), so don't feel you need to overdo it. Pushing your toddler too hard may boost their self-confidence levels in the short term, but may turn out to be a mistake in the longer term for two reasons. First, it could cripple their self-worth by lumbering them with unrealistically high expectations of themselves. If they get used to being head and shoulders above the rest of the class, they may lose confidence in their abilities when the other children begin to catch up. Second, the time you spend teaching them these 'extra' skills in the first place will be time they can't spend learning and rehearsing the skills they *do* need, including vital social skills.

Most child prodigies are overly serious and poor at social interaction. If your four-year-old enters infant school speaking six languages and with a good working knowledge of calculus, the other kids will simply think they're weird. And if they keep themselves to themselves and seem unable to play normally with the other children in the playground, they're well on their way to becoming a social misfit. If they really are a genius, there'll be plenty of time for them to develop their special skills later. If not, you're setting them up for a fall if you encourage them to believe they *are*. Either way, it's a mistake to let even genius get in the way of anything as vitally important as play!

> **Top Tip:** *Primary schools need your toddler to mix, share and pay attention – they don't need a headstart in anything else.*

Curl Up with a Good Book

The most important thing you can give your toddler in the years before they go to school is a committed passion for learning. All toddlers are curious by nature, but some have their curiosity drummed out of them either by drab and uninvolving methods of learning or by exasperated parents who refuse to answer 'why?' for the twenty-eighth time and so unwittingly give them the impression that curiosity is an undesirable trait. The more you can do to encourage your toddler's love for learning and discovery, the better.

119

If they associate learning with fun, activity, excitement and adventure, they'll probably always enjoy learning new things – even when they don't particularly like the new things they're learning! Helping them to love the process of *learning* itself is far more important at this age than *what* they learn.

Take books, for example. Your toddler isn't likely to sit on the floor reading entries in your leather-bound copy of the *Encyclopaedia Britannica*. In fact, if anything they're more likely to scribble on its pages with a wax crayon, or just tear them out to make paper planes – now that's learning! But if they learn from you that books are full of fun and adventure, they'll be far more likely to turn to them later on. As a teenager, they *may* finally read the *Encyclopaedia Britannica* – or even its CD-ROM equivalent!

The input your toddler gets from you now, in other words, may be crucial in determining what they think about reading in later life. If you're enthusiastic about it, they're far more likely to enjoy reading than if you're like Mr Wormwood in Roald Dahl's *Matilda* (recently voted by children as their favourite book). Though Matilda Wormwood is highly intelligent, her 'gormless' father does nothing to foster her passion for reading. Just the opposite, in fact. When she asks him to buy her a book, he refuses point-blank. 'What d'you want a flaming book for?' he asks. 'What's wrong with the telly, for heaven's sake?'

 Top Tip: *At this age, encouraging your child to* **enjoy** *learning, and to see it as an adventure, is far more important than* **what** *they learn.*

'Shall I Read That Again?'

Start your toddler on books by giving them hard-card ones with simple pictures, letters and shapes in them. At one or two, the more indestructible a book is, the better. Read them through with your toddler on your lap, and let them point to things on the pages. Ask them questions about what they see, so they come to understand that books are really interactive. As they get older, give them books that are a little more complicated, with more pages and perhaps a story in them. But make sure they still contain plenty of interesting pictures, and never *expect* your toddler necessarily to be able to read the words, even if they've read the story forty times before. Interacting with the pictures and enjoying the book are far more important for them at this age than reading the contents.

You'll have to develop a thick skin, of course. Whether it's a book they can look through themselves or a more complex story-book for you to read them at bedtime or when they're sitting on the potty, you're sure to be called on to read it over and over and over again. All toddlers have an ability to stomach, and demand, seem-ingly endless repetition. But though it may drive you up the wall, both the repetition and the familiarity it breeds are a vital part of their learning technique. (What's more, as impossible as it may seem right now, you'll eventually remember these moments with joy.)

We all benefit from repetition when learning new things, making use of our familiarity with them to boost our confidence levels: from driving to brain surgery, repetition and familiarity are vital components in the learning process. The only differences with toddlers are that the things they're learning seem to us to be less complicated, and they seem happy for the repetition to be constant and immediate, like an endless loop. They're learning, however, so indulge them, and try not to let your own boredom come out in the tone of voice you use when reading. The more enthusiastic you sound, the more enthusiastic they're likely to be in following along.

Toddlers often use books and stories as a means of enjoying their mum or dad's company – especially when they've heard the story a couple of dozen times before. The soothing voice and familiar tale can have a reassuring, even hypnotic, effect. As a result, they may seem to lose interest in the story and even start doing or fiddling with something else while you're reading. Don't take it personally – it's nothing to do with your skill as a narrator. Instead, stop reading for a minute. If they haven't noticed after a few minutes, it's probably safe for you to assume they've genuinely lost interest, close the book and put it away. But if they object, read on. Remember that the point of the story isn't the plot, but the pleasure of being read to and spending time with you. Above all, don't *force* them to pay attention or interact with the story if they don't want to. The last thing they need is a comprehension test – 'How many pigs were there in Farmer Giles' yard?' 'What did his wife do with his pipe?' That would just undermine all your hours of hard work in trying to get them to enjoy reading books.

Top Tip: *The point of reading a story to your toddler isn't so much the plot as the pleasure they get from being read to by* ***you***.

A Matter of Perspective

When a journalist once asked him to explain his world-famous theory of relativity, Einstein, rather than launching into a detailed scientific explanation of why $e = mc^2$, gave a simple answer: 'When you're courting a nice girl, an hour seems like a second. When you sit on a red-hot cinder, a second seems like an hour. That's relativity.' It's a matter of perspective.

The same is true with toddlers. Remember when you were very young and the days were really long and everything you did was an event in itself that seemed to last an eternity? Well that's where your toddler is now. The world looks bigger and brighter, and a space rocket made from a normal empty washing-up-liquid bottle looks almost like the real thing, and can amuse them for hours. In other words, you don't need a big budget or a cast of thousands to keep them entertained or learning. A little imagination and resourcefulness can go a very long way.

There are just three golden rules to observe when you're playing with your toddler:

- **Always** expect lots of mess, and take whatever precautions (newspaper, plastic sheeting etc.) you think may be necessary to protect your home and furniture.
- **Always** play 'second fiddle', either taking your lead from them or suggesting things they could do next, but never taking over or telling them what to do.
- **Never** criticise or give their work a mental 'score' rating; just let them experiment, give them lots of praise, and worry about things like accuracy and taste when they're older.

 Top Tip: Try to encourage your toddler to **enjoy** learning, and to see it as an adventure.

Fifty Ways to Help Your Toddler Learn

If you're stuck for ways to help your toddler play and learn, then keep reading. Why not try some of the following fifty great ideas?

Sight

1 'I Spy' – always a favourite, this game teaches toddlers to notice

what's around them, as well as what things start (sound, not spelling) with what letters.

2 **Number game** – Getting them to see how many of something (yellow cars, dogs etc.) they can spot will teach recognition as well as simple numbers.

Sound

3 **Singing** – all toddlers love to sing, though they're often more enthusiastic than tuneful! Teach them songs, especially if there are actions, to sing on their own or to singalong with a tape, video or CD.

4 **Animal noises** – whenever they see a cow, horse, cat, dog etc. – either 'live' or in a book – get them to make the right sound.

5 **Weather noises** – get them to make the sound of the wind ('whoosh!') or the rain ('pitter patter, pitter patter').

6 **Percussion** – provided you can sound-proof your kitchen or ensure the neighbours are out, get your toddler to play the drums with saucepan lids and a wooden spoon.

7 **Rhyming** – toddlers love the sound of rhyming words, whether they're taken from Dr Seuss or made up on the spot. Get them to suggest rhymes, not just repeat them.

8 **Accents** – toddlers are good mimics, so make up silly accents for them to copy, especially when you're telling them a story.

Art

9 **Painting** – first with fingers, then with brushes, painting is an old favourite and a source of endless fun. Make sure you keep a representative sample of your toddler's artistic creations until

they're old enough to appreciate them again. Finding out when they're twenty that you kept all their old 'treasures' will help underline your love for them.

10 **Stamping** – though you can buy special ink-stamps, shapes cut in potatoes make cheaper tools for playing with designs.

11 **Colouring** – so long as you don't expect the right colours to go in the right places, you can watch your toddler amuse themselves for a long time colouring in picture outlines with crayons, pens and paints.

12 **Pictures** – as well as pinning them up on walls and fridges, why not buy some cheapish picture frames and frame one or two of their efforts, not just to line the walls of your own house but also to give away as presents to friends and family?

13 **Cards** – folding pieces of cardboard in half and encouraging your toddler to make them into a card to give to someone is a good way of teaching them creativity as well as generosity.

14 **Rubbing** – rubbing a dark crayon on a piece of paper over different surfaces (bubbly, smooth etc.) will help your toddler to learn about texture.

15 **Sculpture** – teach your child to think three-dimensionally by making animals, cars or even pots with either a flour/water dough or, if they're a bit older, modelling clay.

16 **Papier mâché** – provided they're old enough not to eat the paste-glue, papier mâché is a great way of teaching them to build things in layers, perhaps over a pipe-cleaner skeleton.

17 **Collage** – everything from magazine pictures to spaghetti can be used to build up a three-dimensional picture. They may overdo it with the glue, but that just means it'll take longer to dry.

18 **Balloons** – drawing faces or writing words on balloons and then blowing them up will teach your toddler about shape and growth, and be a source of real fun. But supervise them carefully, just in case they try munching on a balloon after it's popped!

Construction

19 **Building blocks** – plastic blocks like Duplo are a great way of teaching your child about height, weight, balance and design. Beware – don't use ones that are small enough to be swallowed.

20 **Cereal or shoe boxes** – with scissors, glue and a coat of paint, these can be turned into anything from tall buildings to dinosaurs to dolls' houses or cars.

21 **Toilet rolls** – with a bit of imagination, empty loo rolls, as well as washing-up-liquid bottles (never use things like empty bleach bottles, as they may have traces of poisons still left in them), can be used to make all sorts of things: Apollo 11, Apollo 12, Apollo 13, or even just telescopes, tunnels and talkie-tubes.

Outside

22 **Park** – outside is a big adventure for your toddler, provided you're there for safety, comfort and companionship. Parks provide fun, freedom and fresh air.

23 **Animals** – from dogs to squirrels and birds, the outside will also bring your child into contact with different types of animals. Why not bring along nuts to feed the birds and squirrels, or bread to feed the ducks?

24 **Swings and slides** – playgrounds can give your toddler immense variety in play, offering them a chance to discover things like gravity, momentum, inertia, speed and centrifugal force: a real science lab! Unlike older children, toddlers usually like their mum or dad to stay close when they play, taking an active interest in their achievements. Most playgrounds now have added safety features like ground-rubber flooring.

25 **Puddle jumping** – very messy, but an awful lot of fun!

26 **Balls** – kicking or rolling large balls to them, and encouraging them to roll or kick them back, will help them with their co-ordination and motor skills.

27 **Tricycles** – sturdier and safer than bicycles for the older toddler, a tricycle helps to teach them steering control and braking distance – eventually! Just make sure they've got a helmet on and aren't showing any exposed skin, as they will come off!

28 **Wigwam** – why not get an old sheet, a broomstick or garden canes and some tent pegs or skewers and set up a wigwam in the back garden (if you have one)?

Bath times

29 **Bath books** – plastic, floating, waterproof bath books combine cleaning the body with stimulating the mind!

30 **Boats** – toys such as ducks or boats help to liven things up, as well as making it a lot easier to coax a reluctant toddler into washing. On top of that, it's educational: for instance, filling the boats up with water teaches them everything they need to know about flotation, buoyancy and the sinking of the *Titanic*!

31 **Eureka!** – ancient Greek physicist Archimedes jumped into his

bath and discovered the principle of volume displacement, but your toddler will learn the same lesson using boats and pots.

32 **Squirties** – you don't need to splash out on expensive toys, as empty shampoo bottles make very good squirties, teaching your child a bit about cause and effect and co-ordination (screwing the cap back on after they've filled them up). Make sure there's a mop on hand and wear a raincoat!

Cookery

33 **Biscuit dough** – by making a batch of biscuit dough or ginger-bread, you can help your toddler enjoy the pleasure of making sculptures they can eat. Wide designs are better than tall ones, as there's less chance of them losing their shape in the oven.

34 **Shapes** – it's not just dough that can be used to make shapes. If you've got shaped biscuit cutters (stars, circles, dinosaurs etc.), you can cut shapes from bread, toast them under the grill (so they hold the shape better) and smother them with jam or honey, or put cheese on top and return them to the grill to melt.

35 **Jam tarts** – one of the easiest recipes for your toddler to make is a jam tart. Simply help them to make the pastry, let them roll it out, cut some rounds with a biscuit cutter, put them into a mini tart-tray, put a dollop of jam in the centre and bake in the oven – a real case of 'Can Cook, Will Cook'!

36 **Pastry portraits** – alternatively, by adding harmless food colouring to the pastry mix, you can create a range of different coloured doughs for your toddler to make faces or other de-signs on a baking tray. Bake when ready.

37 **Food paintings** – encourage them to think creatively about the

food you put in front of them, too. Restaurants put lots of thought into making food look stunning on the plate, so why not create your own food picture? If you're serving bangers and mash, for example, make a stick figure using the sausages for the legs, carrots for the arms, mashed potato for the body and head, and peas for the eyes.

Gardening

38 **Digging holes** – toddlers love digging holes and getting dirty (if you don't have a garden, use a local sandpit). Just ensure they don't dig up your prize-winning roses or eat handfuls of soil, and watch out for dog or cat faeces, which cause infection.

39 **Digging for worms** – snails and worms are the kind of small animal life they're likely to encounter in the garden. It's a healthy source of knowledge about the natural world. Just make sure it doesn't become a snack!

40 **Clearing leaves** – this is the kind of 'helpful' job your toddler can do without specialist skill or much risk of danger, even if you don't have a garden. It'll give them a sense of achievement. Letting them help you with the gardening is a good idea, so long as you don't expect too much and never let them near the lawnmower.

41 **Planting seedlings** – if your toddler shows an interest in being green-fingered, why not give them their own small patch of soil? It won't be as neat or productive as yours, but it'll keep them amused and help them to understand how things grow (though you may need to discourage them from digging things up in order to 'see' the growth). Our kids grew tomatoes in

OKAY SON – MAYBE
WE NEED TO GO BACK
OVER LEAF CLEARING
TECHNIQUES ONE
MORE TIME...

grow-bags. You can also give them a chance to grow seedlings indoors, using something like an old egg box.

Pretending

42 **Dressing up** – whether it's your clothes or special dressing-up clothes, this has always been a big winner with children. They like it almost as much as we do, only we tend to do it much more expensively on the High Street! Let them experiment freely with styles and sizes, as well as with the personalities they adopt once they've got the clothes on.

43 **Colour-coding** – getting your toddler to pick out and then wear clothes of the same basic colour from your wardrobe will be good practice for them in colour recognition. Don't expect them to understand the idea of 'matching outfits', though. Hopefully that's a lesson that'll come in time!

44 **Dolls' party** – whether it's with teddy bears or dolls, encouraging your toddler to create a domestic scene like a tea party

will help them to understand basic table manners.

45 **Playing shop** – money isn't something most toddlers understand, but they can still copy the ritual of handing over money when shopping. So raid your cupboards and let your toddler set up temporary shop with some of the contents. You and the teddy bears may have to be the major customers, but at least the money can be imaginary.

46 **Playing bus** – why not rearrange some of the chairs in your living room or dining room into rows, like on a bus or plane, and encourage your toddler to operate the company – as well as driving/flying the thing, of course.

47 **Playing boat** – alternatively, you could turn your sofa or their bed into a boat. Get them to think of the floor all around as a shark-infested ocean.

48 **Playing elephant** – as every toddler knows, a parent on all fours is really an elephant (or horse), just waiting to be ridden. As long as you're careful they don't fall, this is an excellent way for you to help them control their balance, as well as giving them a chance to get the upper hand for a short while – literally!

Playing House

49 **Washing up** – to a toddler, a household chore can be just as much of an adventure as any game. Our older son Daniel used to love washing up, and always complained if we didn't let him do it. So we did! We gave him a stool, hovered close by and came in with the mop for the kitchen floor afterwards. We sometimes had to do the job again, to our more exacting standards, of course, once he'd finished and left the room. But if

your Duracell-powered youngster wants to help out, let them!

50 **Tidying up** – tidying after playing can also be approached like a game, provided you can summon up enough enthusiasm. Our younger son, Joshua, is still able to generate industrial amounts of mess, but we had to teach him the joys of tidying up when he was about four, after we noticed one day that his bedroom looked like an old World War II bombsite. Sheila, a friend who helps out by doing some cleaning now and then, hadn't been able to drop by for some time, and when we asked Josh how come his room was such a mess, he replied, 'Sheila hasn't been here for six weeks!' It had never occurred to him that he *could*, or *should*, do anything to clear his own clutter. Rather than sternly telling him off, we tried to make it a game – with, to be honest, limited success!

> **Top Tip:** *Imagination and enthusiasm are the vital ingredients in helping your toddler to learn through play.*

Watching the Gogglebox

A last word, about television. Some people think that TV is bad for toddlers, helping stunt their imagination and social skills. A generation ago, many experts even warned that TV was in danger of blunting children's reading skills. But while such scare stories have since turned out to be completely unfounded, it's still worth pointing out that *too much* TV – like too much of *anything* – will have an unhealthy effect on your toddler.

Of course, that doesn't mean there's anything wrong with TV – after all, there's nothing wrong with Shakespeare, but an unrestricted diet of his plays eight hours a day for months on end wouldn't be healthy either. You'll need to restrict how much, and what, your toddler watches. TV, films and CD-ROMs can be a great source of entertainment and information for your toddler, but they're no substitute for playing.

AND AFTER THIS SHOW, A LIFETIME OF BEING A COUCH POTATO.

TV and videos can help spark your toddler's imagination. Programmes like *Teletubbies* and *Sesame Street* can help them enjoy learning; nature and wildlife programmes can keep them enthralled and educated; and films and cartoons can provide *you* with a well-deserved moment of peace and refreshment in another room. But TV is a passive medium, and your toddler needs lots of *active* learning.

134

To make TV less passive and more interactive, you can watch with your toddler, asking them simple questions about what they see and chatting with them about it while it's on or after you switch off. You can also follow it up later with more active forms of play. TV can be used constructively as *part* of play, but it'll never be more than a minor resource. After all, play is more than just learning – it's rehearsing what you've learnt, too.

You wouldn't expect someone to be able to waltz into a top London restaurant and cook like the head chef, having learnt only by watching cookery programmes on television. For all the good they do, they're no substitute for practice and professional training. In just the same way, your toddler won't learn what they need to know in order to make a success of their life just by watching. They need your help and encouragement, and lots and lots of time spent playing as actively and imaginatively as possible.

Top Tip: *Television is a useful supplement to playing, but it's never a substitute for it.*

PART THREE: THE BIG WIDE WORLD

'A Real Social Climber'

How Do I Teach My Toddler to Get On with Others?

'If it moves, it's mine. If it's shiny, it's mine. If it tingles, it's mine. If it's expensive, it's mine. If it rattles, it's mine. If it's small, it's mine. If it's big, it's mine. If you want it, it's mine. If you don't want it, it's still mine. If it's in my room, it's clearly mine. If it's in your room, I'm obviously lending it to you. If it's broken, it's yours.'

That's the way a toddler thinks. As a baby, they had everything they could possibly want on tap. Food, drink, comfort, cleaning and entertainment were all just a short wail away. All that's changed as far as they're concerned is their new-found mobility, which makes it much easier to get what they want and need. Like Emperor Ming in the old *Flash Gordon* series, toddlers are hell-bent on global conquest and absolutely convinced that it's just a case of taking what's rightfully theirs.

When Samuel was two, he proudly showed his grandma a small pile of pennies that, he explained, he'd shortly be depositing in the bank. She was pleased, and asked where he'd got 'such a lot of money'. Without the least hint of guilt, he replied that the pennies had come from *her* purse. He'd opened it up and taken them. But it'd be quite wrong to jump to the conclusion that Sam had intended to steal. He wasn't being deceptive or dishonest. He'd just copied what he'd seen his grandma do on countless occasions.

The problem was that Sam had no understanding of the concept of ownership. So far as he could tell, Grandma's purse was for opening up and taking money out of. No one had taught him that Grandma was the only person legitimately entitled to do this. So not knowing any better, he'd assumed that everything that was Grandma's was, by extension, also his. (To her credit, rather than going ballistic, which wouldn't have done any good, she calmly informed him that 'taking money from other people's purses just isn't something you should do', and Sam learnt another important lesson.)

Top Tip: *Toddlers are naturally selfish – they haven't yet learnt to appreciate the concepts of private property and other people's rights.*

The Whole Truth and Nothing but the Truth

But whether it's innocent or not, such 'selfish' or 'rude' behaviour is highly embarrassing when it's your toddler doing it. I remember

137

taking Emily to church once when she was about three. After the service, the preacher, a personal friend of mine, was saying good-bye to people at the front door, looking as characteristically di-shevelled as I knew he always did – the stereotype of the absent-minded professor. As they filed past, everyone complimented him on his sermon. No one dared mention his appearance – except Emily, who looked him straight in the eyes and asked, 'Who's been chewing your hair?' When your toddler feels such a strong compulsion to speak the truth, the whole truth and nothing but the truth, immediately and extremely loudly, it really is a ground-swallow-me-up moment.

Sometimes, of course, it's not what they *say* that's embarrassing – it's what they *don't say*. Most toddlers seem incapable of saying 'thank you' spontaneously when anyone gives them something, or 'please' when they're asking for something. Try as you might, you just can't get them to be polite. It never seems to occur to them *not* to interrupt, wander off in the middle of a conversation or reach for the things they want without asking. They're instinctively lacking in the social graces.

There's no point in parents complaining about this, however frustrating or blush-inducing it may be. It's just the way toddlers are – a design flaw. They emerge from the womb with no courtesy or thought for others. They're stubborn, whingeing and selfish – all the worst traits of anti-social behaviour. But as their mum or dad, it's your task slowly to teach them how to relate to others. For instance, whenever the situation arises, remind them that it's polite to say 'please' or 'thank you'. Don't force them to say it: that'll only make them see asking and thanking in a negative light. If they don't respond after a gentle prompting – 'What do you say?' – then say it for them and move on. Then explain to them at home why it's important to say 'please' and 'thank you'. When they do say it for themselves, reward them with praise. And try to adopt the same approach when it comes to thoughtless and inconsiderate behaviour. Nagging may produce results in the short term, but it does nothing to create a spirit of consideration and generosity in them for the future.

It may also help to explain to your toddler the effect courtesy can have on other people. Rather than frogmarching them up to granny at Christmas or on their birthday and ordering them to thank her for their present, why not ask them, 'Are you going to say thank you for your present? Granny would *like* that.'

Of course, none of this will do any good if they never see you minding your manners. Like it or not, your toddler's Number One role model is you, and they observe your behaviour very closely. If they see you being thoughtful and polite most of the time, they're a lot more likely to adopt this kind of behaviour themselves. On the other hand, if they never hear you say 'please' or 'thank you', what motivation do they have to be courteous? What's more, if you never ask them to do things politely, or thank them when they do – but always bark orders at them instead – they'll come to see that politeness and consideration are virtues you preach but don't practise.

 Top Tip: Don't nag your toddler to say 'please' and 'thank you' – give them a firm and clear example to follow by doing it yourself.

The Blood Supply to Your Leg

Sometimes, of course, toddlers just don't say anything at all when they meet someone they're not that familiar with. Instead, they clam up and cling to the back of your leg so hard that it threatens to cut off the blood supply. Suddenly your two-year-old Terminator has become shy.

Shyness is another natural trait for toddlers, though opinion is divided about its merits. On the one hand, there's something healthy about a toddler's caution with strangers, especially given society's increased awareness of 'stranger danger'. Gone are the 'golden days' when you could leave the front door unlocked and be confident that your little munchkin would be safe. On the other hand, by encouraging a toddler's shyness, parents can risk impairing their social skills and even condemning them to a life of relative isolation and loneliness.

In fact, however, the 'golden days' were never that golden. While it's true that people used not to have to lock their doors in some parts of the country, it's not true that their kids were necessarily any safer then than now. 'Stranger danger' is, of course, terrifying and real, but the threat of abuse is and always has been much greater from a friend or family member than from a stranger. What's more, if you try to protect your toddler by allowing them to hide away from other people, even if it's only behind your leg, you'll be depriving them of the chance to develop the vital social skills and self-confidence they'll need if they're going to be able to protect themselves or make friends in future. They'll always need some kind of 'leg' to hide behind. So teaching toddlers to get on with others isn't just a survival trick for parents – aimed at eventually ending those awkward moments when they forget to say 'please' or 'thank you', or interrupt a conversation, or walk off with granny's purse, or insist on telling the whole truth at an inappropriate moment – it's also a survival trick for the toddlers themselves.

Shyness is inevitable at first, of course, but it's important not to let it turn into a habit. If you're at home and someone comes to see you, encourage your toddler to say hello to the visitor, preferably looking at them while they do so, then praise them for doing the right thing and leave them to play quietly on their own. Don't insist on anything more – your toddler isn't a showpiece, and they'll quickly get bored by adult conversation. But if you're out and about, and you can't let them run around on their own, pick them up, holding them in your arms or sitting them on your shoulders if possible, so they don't feel excluded from your conversation. Don't leave them to hang around your leg.

Above all, don't talk for too long, or your toddler will not only begin to associate strangers with boredom, they'll also start to resent the interference because it deprives them of your attention. If you *need* to talk about something with the person, either invite them round or arrange to chat with them over the phone. After all, your toddler won't learn how to be considerate from you if you don't show any consideration to them!

The most important ingredient, however, is self-confidence. The more your toddler learns to believe that you love them with no strings attached, the less shy they'll be in the presence of strangers. And because they know you love them unconditionally, they'll handle being disciplined a lot better, which should help you tackle those awkward little moments when they decide to use company as an excuse to forget what you've taught them and act up.

 Top Tip: Help your toddler get over their shyness by giving their self-confidence a boost.

The Elastic Family

The most convenient strangers to practise on, of course, are your parents and in-laws, wider family and close friends – anyone you have a good, trusting and relaxed relationship with. They're the most 'intimate strangers' your toddler will probably get to know outside your immediate family for some years. You trust them, and once your toddler has picked this up, they'll trust them, too.

If they're still alive and available, grandparents usually love to spend time with their grandchildren, so your toddler is bound to approve of them – who wouldn't approve of such a captive and responsive audience? What's more, having been parents once already, grandparents often have both a knowledge and a confidence born of experience, which will give your toddler an instinctive feeling of comfort and security.

Seeing grandparents or other close family and friends on a fairly regular basis will help your toddler practise their manners and consideration on a 'soft target', and help them to understand that there's more to family than just you and them. It can also be good for you, of course, since many friends and relations are only too happy to baby-sit every now and then. This will help your toddler get on with others even more, as well as giving you a much-needed night or even weekend off, safe in the knowledge that your toddler is being well looked after. (It won't even matter, and could even help, if they spoil them a bit.)

Top Tip: As trusted 'intimate strangers', your toddler's grandparents are an ideal 'soft target' for teaching them to get on with others.

The Good Childminder Guide

Sometimes, of course, family members or very close friends aren't available to look after your toddler when you need a break or have to go out to work. At times like this, when you need a baby-sitter or a childminder, it can be hard to know what to look for in a prime candidate. Most of the time, your choice will be limited by all sorts of practical considerations. The person you choose needs to be: available, affordable, relatively local, appropriate, and someone your toddler won't mind too much being left with. All this can reduce your options drastically.

The best kind of baby-sitter is someone both you and your toddler know and trust – a friend or another parent. Apart from anything else, it's likely to be easier and a lot cheaper. But if this isn't possible, you'll have to look for someone with whom the arrangement will be more business-based. Ask around to see if there's anyone your friends or relatives would recommend. Don't be afraid to ask awkward questions: they should be happy to tell you what experience and qualifications they have, and mature enough not to take it personally. In fact, your inquisitiveness should help them respect you and your house rules.

In looking for a good baby-sitter, it's a good idea to make sure they're over sixteen (otherwise they may lack the maturity and experience needed to cope well if anything goes wrong). If possible, invite them over beforehand as a kind of 'rehearsal' to see how they relate to your toddler: are they sensitive, considerate, attentive, confident, but firm? A rehearsal gives both the sitter and your toddler a chance to get to know each other a bit. But it also gives you an opportunity to reassure yourself about them, helping you to relax while you're out. Make sure they have an emergency phone number to reach you; a First Aid kit; spare nappies or underwear and bed linen for your toddler if they wet the bed or themselves; and appropriate food and drink in case they or your toddler are hungry.

When it comes to choosing a childminder to look after your toddler during the day, it's worth doing a little extra checking to make sure that they have the right qualifications (approved by your local authority) and that their references are reliable. Look round their facilities (check for both resources and general safety, whether it's their home or somewhere else) and make sure that they aren't trying to look after too many children at once. Talk to them about what you want and what your toddler likes doing, and confirm that they're happy with that. It's a good idea for them to give you a 'diary' of everything your toddler does and eats during the day. That way you can keep a track of any 'significant milestones' they've achieved, and ensure that you don't duplicate either their diet or their activities on your return. Check in advance they'd be willing to do this, and are prepared to make any changes you ask for in the routine. Don't be afraid to agree a 'probationary' period, after which time you can review things and decide whether or not to continue the arrangement (either you or they may feel it's best to look elsewhere).

Above all, make sure you brief them well about bedtimes and behaviour: if you don't tell them you want something done in a particular way, or what your code of conduct is, then you've only yourself to blame if they do something you don't like. It's up to *you* to ensure that the values your toddler learns from those you appoint to care for them are values you're comfortable with.

 Top Tip: When you need a baby-sitter or childminder, find one you feel comfortable with, but don't assume they can ever take **your** place.

Joining the Rat Race

For the first two or three years of their life, your toddler will be mostly self-contained. They'll usually be quite happy playing by themselves, and if they do choose a playmate, it's more likely to be you than anyone their own age. If you put two two-year-olds in a room together and watch them play, you're unlikely to see much interaction between them. They like the company, but toddlers of that age don't so much play *with* each other as *beside* each other.

But around about the age of three, this starts to change and they begin to be far more interested in playing with their peers. This marks an important step in their ability to form relationships with other people, and it's a good idea to give them the opportunity to build on this by enrolling them in a nursery. Look for one that's registered, well resourced, relatively near, not too expensive and not too formal. Inspect the safety of the building and play areas, ascertain the teacher–pupil ratio (which should be at least 1:4 for children between the ages of two and three, and 1:8 for children between the ages of three and five), and talk to the teachers to make sure you feel confident with them. Ask to sit in and observe, either before you take your toddler along or on the first few sessions (many places insist you do this before they'll agree to accept your child). If you don't like what you see or the attitude of the staff, move on and look for somewhere else.

Whether they're two, three or four, toddlers learn mostly by playing. This means that a good purpose-built nursery, or school nursery facility, will provide a play-centred schedule, where toddlers are encouraged to enjoy doing their own thing most of the time, as well as a smattering of group activities such as stories or sing-songs. A nursery atmosphere should be fun, relaxed and informal, with a high staff–pupil ratio. On no account should your toddler be expected to sit still and 'perform' academically – this type of 'nursery' is likely to do them more harm than good. A nursery should promote fun, friendship, sharing and stories. It should be about learning through *playing with others*. A toddler who plays is a toddler who prepares. A toddler who isn't allowed to play is a toddler who isn't given enough time to prepare themselves for the difficult road ahead. If a nursery's atmosphere is too formal, not only will your toddler be deprived of vital playing time, they may also start to associate learning with formality, not fun, which could seriously backfire in terms of their academic progress a few years down the line.

 Top Tip: Nursery school is about learning through **playing** with others, so make sure you look for somewhere with a play-centred schedule.

'Lights, Camera, Action ...'

Never assume, just because your toddler has been cared for and stimulated by a childminder or nursery all day, or watched over by a baby-sitter all evening, that you're off the hook as far as spending time with them is concerned. Other people can support your role but they can never supplant it. To your child, you're indispensable. *You* have the main responsibility for raising your toddler. It's *your* love, time and attention they most need. Never forget it.

In Hollywood, it's traditional for big stars to have both stand-ins and stunt-doubles when they're making a film. The two jobs are very different from one another. A stunt-double is someone who substitutes for the star on film when a dangerous stunt is called for;

if it's made well, the audience never knows a switch has been pulled and assumes that the person they see performing the stunt is the star themselves. A stand-in, by contrast, never even makes it into the film: their role is to stand in for the star while all the lighting and camera angles are being set up. This enables the technical crew to make sure things are set up at the right height, depth and focus, but at the same time lets the star arrive at the last minute, focused and ready for the scene rather than worn down by two hours of waiting for everything to be set up just right. Both stunt-doubles and stand-ins are vital parts of virtually any film, and the star couldn't do their job without them. But at the end of the day, it's the star that audiences want to see.

In many ways, a baby-sitter is like a stand-in. If all goes well, your toddler never really sees them much, but they give you a chance to get some much-needed refreshment so you'll be more focused and ready for what lies ahead. A childminder or nursery school is like a stunt-double, substituting for you at critical moments. There's even a cast of supporting actors – friends, brothers and sisters, grandparents etc. – to give things a bit of interest and variety so you're not up there on your own. But as important as all these ingredients are, *you're* the star in your toddler's life. *You're* the one they're longing to see.

Top Tip: *Other people won't make it less important for you to spend time with your toddler – if anything, they'll make it even **more** important!*

'Well, He Started It!'

How Do I Cope with Jealousy
and Sibling Rivalry?

In Disney's film, *Toy Story*, Andy's birthday and Christmas Day are annual nightmares for most of his toys. They know only too well that the arrival of an expensive new toy would undoubtedly turn some of them into garage sale fodder. Only Mr Potatohead (desperately hoping for the arrival of a *Mrs* Potatohead) and cowboy Woody (convinced that as Andy's favourite toy he couldn't *possibly* be replaced) dare to be optimistic. So when Woody is suddenly shunted off the bed to make way for a new toy, Buzz Lightyear, he becomes so insanely jealous that he even plots to get rid of Buzz!

New arrivals always cause problems, because they affect the equilibrium of a household. A friend of mine warns couples who're about to give birth for a second time, or families who're about to become instantly bigger through the addition of stepchildren, that a new arrival has the potential to stir up as much jealousy as joy. As the boss of a charity that works with families up and down the country, he's seen the pattern repeat itself over and over again. 'How would you feel,' he asks the couples, 'if your partner came home one day with a new spouse and told you how pleased you should be that you now had a co-husband or co-wife? Wouldn't you be more likely to see them as a rival for your partner's affection? Well that's how your toddler will feel if you present them with a new sister or brother but don't work hard to ensure you're still giving *them* all the love, time and attention they need.'

A new baby brother or sister is a potential threat as far as your toddler is concerned. Having got used to the dynamics of a relationship that was just you and them, they suddenly have to come to terms with all sorts of changes in routine and response. Of course, some toddlers welcome the intrusion, but others feel vulnerable, uncertain as to how they fit into the equation now that the family has multiplied. Seeing you lavish love and attention on their brother or sister, they may wonder if there'll still be enough left for them or if the new arrival means that they'll now have to make do with a smaller slice of the cake.

If your toddler *is* feeling vulnerable, it's vital for you to make sure you give them all the reassurance they need that you haven't stopped loving them – and couldn't stop loving them even if you tried. Just because there's someone new in the house doesn't mean you love them any less. Love *isn't* like a cake that you have to divide between people. It's new and different and complete for *everyone* you care about. So make sure you think carefully about how you apportion your time and attention – to a toddler, appearance is reality. It's no good telling them you love them as much as ever if they can't see it in your behaviour.

151

Top Tip: *Your toddler may well feel vulnerable if your family grows, so give them all the reassurance they need that you love them as much as ever.*

Chalke's Law

Vying for the lion's share of your attention isn't the only reason brothers or sisters don't always get along. Tension can be caused by tiredness, frustration or simply the desire on your toddler's part to stretch their muscles and try it on. But there are also three other main causes for sibling rivalry: the closeness of a home environment; the emergence of a healthy competitive streak; and that ever-present green-eyed monster, jealousy.

Over the twenty odd years I've been involved with young people, both professionally and personally as a dad, I've slowly come to realise a basic and universal truth of family life – Chalke's Law: *no matter how large your house is, it's never big enough*. But this is nothing to do with physical limits – it's about 'personal space'. Many of the fights that happen between brothers and sisters are more to do with personal issues they're facing than with *inter*personal ones. The problem is that, in the hothouse environment of a family, one child may not feel they have the space they need to deal with personal pressures, tensions and worries without causing massive disruption to the rest of the family. However spacious your home, your family's a confined group, which means that you're eventually bound to take out your problems on someone else.

And this isn't just true of your children. Tension is a spreadable disease: it can pass from one family member to another in seconds. Which means that if *you're* tense, worried or frustrated by the hassles of work, home or everyday life, the chances are that your kids will soon become tense, worried or frustrated, too. And there's lots to be tense, worried or frustrated about when you've got a barrel-load of toddlers.

I remember once, when Emily was three, she started crying loudly and persistently just after Corni and I had got into bed. She wasn't very well, and I knew we couldn't just leave her. Corni was exhausted after taking care of Daniel, who was about one and teething, and it was my turn to get up in the night to try to sort Emily out. But no sooner had I picked her up than she vomited all over me (including my hair!), herself and the bed. Bleary-eyed, I changed her pyjamas and her bedding, settled her down again, tucked her into bed, kissed her goodnight and then had a shower before finally clambering back into bed myself. An hour or so later, she was crying again. I got up a second time to see what was wrong and couldn't believe it when she threw up over me *again*. Once more I had to change her pyjamas and bedding, tuck her up, kiss her goodnight, and then clean myself up.

When she cried again two hours later, vomiting over everything for a third time, I had to pinch myself just to make sure I wasn't dreaming – how long could this nightmare go on? But no sooner had my head touched the pillow after going through the same rigmarole once more than the alarm went off, spelling the start of another working day. Not surprisingly, having had my sleep interrupted three times, I wasn't in the best of moods. Neither was Emily. And pretty soon, neither were Corni or Daniel. I escaped to the office as quickly as I could, leaving Corni to the mercy of a pair of grumpy toddlers constantly setting each other off. Happy families? Not a chance!

Of course, having more than one toddler is tricky even when they're not ill. The amount of preparation needed just for a trip to the shops is exhausting, and it's even worse if you have to take them somewhere formal, like a wedding. It's easy to see why some African tribes used to have a strict community rule: never have more children than there are adults to carry them. The idea was that they could carry all their children to safety quickly if their village was ravaged by fire or attacked by a neighbouring tribe. But this high adult–child ratio had another big advantage, of course: families were always manageable – literally! Even though they were usually quite large and composed of three or four generations, when things got tough, there were always other adults around to help out.

 Top Tip: *However large your home is, it's never big enough to contain all the tensions of family life – so some sibling rivalry is inevitable.*

'And the Winner Is ...'

Some sibling tension is caused by toddlers' built-in competitive streak. Competition is an inevitable fact of life: sometimes good, sometimes bad. From sports and game shows to job interviews and advertising, it's part of almost everything we do. There's no way to protect your child from competition completely, nor should you want to. If you don't teach them to handle competition *now*, both winning and losing, they'll be at a real disadvantage when they encounter it at school, if not before. Hiding your kids away from competition isn't the answer. In the long run, it'll leave them under-prepared for life. By far the better policy is to provide a safe environment in which they can experience all the ups and downs of competition without getting badly hurt, and learn to cope with it all.

So rather than trying to squash all their battles and arguments – and solve their problems *for* them – it's better for you to take a back seat and interfere only if things start to get out of hand. Whenever possible, let them learn to resolve their own tensions and problems. Think of it as being a bit like a tennis match, where your children are the players and you're the umpire. Your job isn't to stop them from confronting each other or battling it out: it's simply to ensure that they stick to the rules and play fair.

Always look before you leap. Just like any umpire, your job is to remain impartial. If you didn't see something with your own eyes, either refuse to make a judgment or get both sides of the story before you make up your mind. Though some squabbles really *are* what they appear to be, the majority aren't. When Corni and I went into the back garden one day and found that next door's rotten fence had been almost completely dismantled, our first thought was that the neighbours had finally decided to do something about it. But on closer inspection, we found that the rotten slats were left haphazardly on *our* side of the fence, that *our* flowerbeds (to use the word rather loosely) were trampled, and that Daniel – who was three at the time – was standing there with a satisfied look on his face! Acting on the facts as we saw them, we punished him accordingly. Unfortunately, what we *didn't* know was that he'd only been acting on orders from his older, 'wiser' sister Emily, who'd assured him that we and the neighbours would be delighted!

More often than not, fights between siblings are a case of six of one and half a dozen of the other. So if one of your toddlers comes to you complaining that the other one hit them, and you take their story at face value, you run the risk of making a premature and unfair judgment – in time that'll gradually undermine your authority and relationship with them both. The one thing that's absolutely guaranteed to produce an unhappy home is when parents seem to favour one child more than another, because it's vital for all your children to know you love them equally, for who they are and with no strings attached.

At the same time, however, it's important that you don't get *equal* treatment confused with *identical* treatment. They're not necessarily the same thing. Some issues will obviously be the same across the board, like not getting down from table before the meal is over, not lying, not treading mud throughout the house, being polite, always saying 'please' and 'thank you' etc. But there are also lots of things that'll vary because each of your children is different from the others: different personalities and (unless they're twins) different ages, just for starters. That means that, though your goal may be the same, your method for achieving it will differ from child to child.

The only real way to get to the roots of sibling rivalry and ensure that you're fair and equal in how you treat your kids is to spend *time* with them – and not just when there's a crisis. If the only time you really spend time talking to your toddler is when they've done something wrong, they'll learn that the best way to get high-quality, one-on-one attention is by making trouble. Spending time with each child on a regular basis is a wise investment because you'll get to know a lot more about them – which will help you anticipate some of the potential flashpoints before they arise. And by giving them your undivided attention, you'll also eliminate a high percentage of the squabbles before they have a chance to start. If you spend individual time with each of your children, they'll know you love *them* enough to want to be with them, and that's bound to reduce the amount of rivalry between them.

 Top Tip: You can't hide your children from competition, but you **can** prepare them for it by acting as an impartial referee.

Old Green Eyes Is Back

Sometimes, of course, even strenuous equality and even-handedness can backfire. Toddlers are still struggling to come to terms with difficult concepts like sharing, generosity, human rights (other people's, that is!) and patience. As a result, they may seem totally impervious to the idea that their brother or sister's new toy or tricycle isn't theirs to do with as they please. Though it's a phase

157

they'll grow out of as they gradually learn to respect other people's wishes and property, and become more able to manage their emotions, it can drive parents up the wall while it lasts. There's no real remedy or course of action you can take: your toddler just has to learn that they can't have everything they want. It's part of life, and it's far better for them to learn it *now*, in a safe home environment, than *later* the hard way.

When three-year-old Jack and his five-year-old brother Charlie were each given a toy car by their grandfather, everyone thought they'd be happy. Unfortunately, Jack was far from happy. Although the cars were the same size, the same make and made the same sound, they weren't quite identical, and Jack felt wronged. It seemed clear to him that his brother's yellow sports car was *much* nicer than his blue one. But as luck would have it, for once in their lives he and Charlie agreed, so there was absolutely no chance of a swap, and the little yellow car became a source of endless friction. Jack played with it whenever his brother wasn't around, and sulked whenever Charlie angrily claimed it back. Their mum considered taking it away or 'accidentally' breaking it, but decided that such a move would only make things worse: rather than resenting each other, they'd end up resenting *her*. So she decided just to let things run their course: either Jack would grow out of his selfishness or the little yellow car would break. In the end, it was both, at roughly the same time.

In our house, the cause of jealous tension and rivalry wasn't a car – it was a cat. Friday came to us when our youngest child, Joshua, was a boisterous four-year-old. Most toddlers react in one of two extreme ways toward cats: they're either petrified, or else try to hug them to death. With Joshua, it was love at first sight. Unfortunately, love and gentleness didn't go hand in hand, and within hours a somewhat roughed-up kitten appeared to have vowed never to have anything more to do with Joshua. His was the one room Friday never went into, and the one bed Friday never slept on. The problem was that, to Joshua, the blame for this boycott rested entirely with his brother and sisters. At four, with his logic not yet firing on all cylinders, all he understood was that Emily, Daniel and Abigail got Friday's attention, but *he* didn't. As with Jack and the little yellow car, there was nothing to be done but wait it out. Six years later, Joshua's jealousy has subsided – nevertheless, Friday *still* very rarely goes into his room!

 Top Tip: *When jealousy causes sibling rivalry, the best course of action is often **no** course of action – your toddler has to learn they can't have everything they want.*

'There's No Place Like Home'

An A to Z of Toddler Troubleshooting

Some friends sent us one of those Christmas newsletters last year recounting what they'd been up to over the previous twelve months. Letters like that are often dull, but not this one – it was riveting! And most of it was taken up describing the antics of their two-year-old son, James.

> James is very active, and has incredible energy resources. He wakes at about five most mornings. He *runs* everywhere, and can't be left without close supervision for more than a few seconds. Some of his more memorable 'activities' during the year include: dialling 999 on at least two occasions; igniting the gas hob; discovering the electricity meter in our holiday cottage and switching off the mains supply – we thought we'd had a power failure; finding the keys to Nick's car and starting the engine; stealing shoes from Marks and Spencer; stealing a CD from a music store and activating the alarm; eating half a box of continental chocolates (not his) which were in the fridge – he'd managed to open two childproof, but obviously not

James-proof, fridge locks in order to achieve this; and opening the foil lids on a pack of twelve yoghurts while Alice was unloading the weekly groceries and pouring the contents over the sofa.

He enjoys interior design, and is particularly skilled at peeling off wallpaper borders and drawing all over newly wallpapered walls with a thick black marker pen. He speaks no intelligible words of English, but talks jargon and communicates well in other ways. He's been clinically assessed as highly intelligent, excessively active and strong-willed. Needless to say, he's hard work. We feel constantly tired but love him very much.

All toddlers are hard work and extremely time-consuming. That's why the last chapter of this book is a kind of 'ready resource'. Rather than adding new information, the aim here is simply to provide a quick-reference summary of some of the main trouble-spots dealt with in the rest of this book. For convenience, it's arranged in an A–Z format.

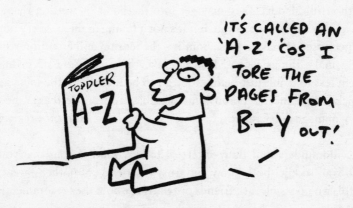

AD(H)D. Attention Deficit Hyperactivity Disorder is the recent name for what used to be called 'hyperactivity'. You can tell if your toddler is hyperactive, as they'll be exactly like every other toddler – only more so! So the 'treatment' is also exactly the same as for every other toddler, only more so: routine, love, praise, discipline, play and lots and lots of attention. ADHD isn't normally diagnosed until the age of about six, so drug therapy with stimulants such as Ritalin – which makes life more tolerable for everyone else but does little for the toddler themselves – isn't an option. Consult your GP if you're worried. SEE CHAPTER 5

Bed-wetting. Up to 10 per cent of all five-year-olds still wet the bed, and it *can* continue up to age eight. Stress can cause bed-wetting to persist, or return if your toddler has previously gone dry, so try to find out if anything's upsetting them. If not, the cause could be 'slow' development (*not* a problem) or habit: toddlers, like adults, wake or nearly wake several times in the night; if they wake with a full bladder, they may get into the habit of wetting themselves. It's frustrating to you, but it's not a failing in them, so try not to get upset or make a fuss about it – the tension and attention will only make things worse. Instead, take the precaution of giving them less to drink just before they go to bed, clean up the mess as quickly and unceremoniously as possible, and praise them when they manage a dry night. SEE CHAPTER 5

Childminders and Baby-sitters. The best kind is someone you and your toddler both know and trust – a friend or another parent. If this isn't possible, ask friends or relatives whom they recommend.

With a childminder, check qualifications and references. Inspect the facilities and make sure they're not trying to look after too many toddlers at once. Tell them what you want and what your toddler likes doing. Try it for a 'probationary' period. Ask them to give you a 'diary' of everything your toddler does and eats, and explain your code of conduct and anything you want done in a special way. It's up to *you* to ensure that the values your toddler learns during the day are values you're comfortable with.

Try to ensure a baby-sitter is over sixteen, and if possible have a 'rehearsal' first to see how they relate to your child: are they sensitive, considerate, attentive, confident, but firm? Give them an emergency contact phone number; a First Aid kit; spare nappies, underwear and bed linen; and food and drink for them and your toddler.   SEE CHAPTER 7

Dinnertime Dramas. If your toddler is having trouble ensuring that their spoon makes it to their mouth without dropping the contents on the floor, stay calm. They either need to fine-tune their 'fine motor' skills or they're conducting a science experiment on gravity. And if you think they're being deliberately naughty, you *don't* want to reward their misbehaviour with your anger. Resist the temptation to play aeroplanes or trains: they'll like it, which means they'll do the same thing again as a way of saying 'encore'.

Food is rarely worth going to war over. If they consistently refuse certain types of food, don't cook them – give them something they will eat instead. If all they seem to eat is junk food, don't buy it for them. If they won't eat what's put in front of them, let them go hungry. They can afford to miss a meal – their self-preservation instincts are strong, so they *won't* starve. If they're hungry later, give them either the food they turned down or a healthy snack (*never* reward them with a chocolate bar).   SEE CHAPTERS 4 AND 5

Expectations. Before they have children, most parents think they can do a near-perfect job. But as they hold their new-born babe in their arms, their confidence evaporates. Rather than being a realistic goal, perfection becomes a massive burden. And just when they think they've mastered most of the survival techniques, their child goes mobile and dramatically ups the ante. It's important, therefore, to realise that you're not a substandard parent. The truth is, there's no sure-fire way to raise a happy child. There's not even any guarantee that what works with one toddler one day will work with the same toddler – or any other toddler – the next. Parenting techniques are as individual as the children themselves. This book explains the key principles, but most of it's a matter of trusting your own judgment.   SEE CHAPTER 1

Fears and Phobias. To a toddler, the world is full of the unknown and unfriendly. A one-year-old is likely to be relatively fearless – except for the anxiety of being separated from *you* – but a two- or three-year-old will become much more prone to fear and distress. It's the flipside of their imagination. They need imagination to make sense of the world, but don't yet have the kind of logical framework to differentiate between fact and fantasy.

There's no point in telling your toddler off for their fears, and limited value in rational explanations as they don't think rationally. If you do give explanations, a reassuring tone of voice will communicate more than a logic. Above all, never belittle them for being afraid or tell them to 'grow up'. Look for practical solutions and give lots of attention (but be careful they don't prolong or concoct phobias just to get your attention).   SEE CHAPTER 5

Grandparents. Even if they live ten thousand miles away and can only communicate by sending the odd letter, tape or videotape message, toddlers benefit from contact with their grandparents. Along with close friends, and other close family members such as uncles and aunts, they're the most 'intimate strangers' your toddler will probably know outside their immediate family for some years. The contact will help them practise their manners and consideration on a 'soft target', and make them see there's more to family than just you and them. Most grandparents *love* spending time with their grandchildren. What's more, having been parents once already, they often have knowledge and confidence born of experience. (It won't matter, and may even help, if they spoil them a bit, provided *you* don't spoil them and there's a consistent, comforting code of conduct whenever you're around.)   SEE CHAPTER 7

Health. If you're worried about your toddler's health, behaviour, or development, consult your GP. Don't worry about the danger of 'pestering' them: most GPs would far rather see a toddler unnecessarily than risk failing to detect a problem in its early, usually more treatable, stages. Besides, by reassuring you that your toddler is OK, they're helping to protect *you* against the onset of stress- or worry-related illness.   SEE CHAPTER 5

Individuality. Toddlerhood is the time in which children acquire the foundations of their personality and temperament. Though some elements of their personality and appearance come down to them through their genes, most are slowly created by how they 'respond to their environment' – in other words, what happens to them and how they're treated, as well as the choices they make. The lessons you teach them, and the support and attention you give them, will help them later in life – the more time and tenderness you invest in them in these formative years, the more chance you'll give them of growing up as a happy, mature, self-confident adult, aware of their unique strengths and weaknesses.   SEE CHAPTER 1

Juggling Roles. It's easy to blame your job or domestic situation for the lack of time you have to spend with your toddler. But the truth is that it's more to do with your *personality* than your profession. You generally *can* spend more time with them if you want to, and if you're disciplined enough to make some tough choices. As they say, 'Where there's a will, there's a way'. Don't imagine a 'right moment' will come along when you'll have the time you need to spend with your toddler – instead, start small and start *now*! And remember: investing time in your toddler isn't just the *right* thing to do, it's also highly rewarding!   SEE CHAPTER 2

Kicking the Habit. From biting and nose-picking to thumb-sucking and breath-holding, toddlers acquire a host of bad habits from their surroundings and instincts. Some, like playing with their private parts, are just a harmless extension of their curiosity, and making a big deal over them will just make things worse. Others, such as thumb-sucking, can give real comfort and joy. With a dangerous habit, you'll need to take a firm line, telling them 'no' and reinforcing this by doing something that deprives them of your attention (e.g., putting them in a corner of the room for a few minutes). SEE CHAPTER 5

Learning. Toddlers mainly learn by playing – it's how they learn about themselves, their body, their environment and their place in the world, as well as being a vital rehearsal for it. There's no part of their development – physical, mental, emotional, social, personal, linguistic and artistic – that isn't helped by their playing. A child who doesn't play enough, doesn't adequately develop the skills they need to get on top of life. More formal ways of learning are inappropriate. The golden rule is: if your toddler can't learn it in play, they don't need to learn it yet. SEE CHAPTER 6

Morality. As a parent, it's your responsibility to instil in your toddler a 'code of conduct', helping them develop an awareness of how to behave properly. They look to you for guidance, and rely on you to keep them safe. The code you teach them will guide them through life, not just as a child, but also – with modifications – as an adult. That's why it's vital for your moral 'code' to be consistent. It's hard enough for a toddler to 'crack' the code in the first place, but if you keep changing it on them – letting them do something one day and punishing them for it the next – they're bound to end up scared and confused. And they'll be at a disadvantage when it comes to knowing what to expect and how to behave around other people. SEE CHAPTER 4

Naivety. Many of the things toddlers do aren't done out of mischievousness, but simply because they have an almost total lack of common sense and little understanding of cause and effect. To a toddler, the 'long-term future' is at the most sixty seconds from now, so imagining the consequences of an action is almost impossible. What's more, they have no experience to fall back on and only just enough hand–eye co-ordination to be lethal – both to themselves and anything breakable. Like an unguided missile, they're full of energy but with absolutely no idea where they're going. So never expect too much of a toddler's 'logic' – they haven't had time to develop it yet. SEE CHAPTER 4

Obedience. There's no Universal Handbook for teaching your toddler obedience and self-discipline. Every toddler is different, so what works with one might not work with another. To know how to discipline your toddler, you'll need to make time to get to know them inside out. This will also help you develop the kind of strong, loving relationship with them that'll make your discipline more effective. The secret of good discipline isn't the techniques you use on your child, but the strength of your relationship. If they don't know you love them then whatever techniques you use, you'll be fighting a losing battle. SEE CHAPTER 4

Potty Training. When they're born, your toddler's on/off tap isn't developed enough to let them to go to the loo voluntarily. They only start gaining control over their bowel and bladder when they're between eighteen months and two years old. Before this age they're usually oblivious to 'what goes in must come out'.

Put your toddler on the potty as soon as they're able to sit up –
but before they're able to crawl off it again! Don't expect miracles
– they'll need plenty of time to get used to the idea. The first milestone is just getting them to sit comfortably on the potty. The rest
will come later. Routine is vital, so make potty time an after-meal
ritual – this is a good time to do it since most toddlers soil their
nappies after eating anyway, not through choice but as a reflex action. The more relaxed you make it, the better – they need to see it
as a natural part of life, not a test. As with all toddler behaviour,
give lots of praise when they do well, as this will encourage them to
repeat the triumph. Never chastise them for failure. Instead, downplay mishaps and play up achievements. Above all, don't let your
frustration show if they won't sit still or if they soil their nappy
moments after an unproductive potty session.

Once your child is out of nappies, immediacy is vital. 'Holding
it in' for long is beyond their abilities, so look for somewhere fast if
they say they need to go. Don't tell them off for not having thought
about it earlier: they haven't learnt to think that far ahead yet. It's
much better to encourage them to go anyway beforehand than
blame them afterwards.   SEE CHAPTER 5

Quantity Time. Toddlers spell 'love' T-I-M-E, judging their importance on the *quantity* and *quality* of time we spend with them.
This makes a lot of sense – after all, if you love someone, you want
to spend as much time with them as you can. Being around them
says, 'I'm comfortable with you. I enjoy being with you. I love you.'
Sometimes you only have to be there in the room while they play on
their own. At other times, you need to be more actively involved in

what they're doing. All toddlers are 'attention junkies', which means you'll often have to stop what you're doing and look at what they're doing instead. It's not enough to be paying attention – your toddler has to *know* you're paying attention. SEE CHAPTER 2

Reading. Few under-fives can 'sight read', so your toddler won't sit on the floor reading the *Encyclopaedia Britannica*. But if they learn to see books as fun and adventurous, they'll like them more in later life. So start your toddler on books by giving them hard-card ones with simple pictures, letters and shapes in them. For one- or two-year-olds, the more indestructible books are, the better. Read them with your toddler on your lap, and let them point to things on the pages. Ask them questions about what they see, so they realise that books are interactive. As they get older, give them books that are a bit more complicated, with more pages and per-haps a story in them. But make sure they still have lots of interest-ing pictures, and never *expect* your toddler to read the words, even if they've heard the story forty times before. Interacting with the pictures and enjoying the experience are far more important for them at this age than reading the contents.

Toddlers often use books and stories to enjoy their mum or dad's company – especially when they know the story. The soothing voice and familiar tale can have a reassuring, even hypnotic, effect. As a result, they may lose interest in the story and even start doing or fiddling with something else while you're reading. Don't take it personally – it's nothing to do with your skill as a narrator. Remember that the point of the story isn't the plot, but the pleasure of spending time with you. Above all, don't *force* them to pay

170

attention – that'll undermine all your hard work in trying to get them to enjoy reading books.　　　SEE CHAPTER 6

Smacking. Every parent must decide for themselves whether or not it's right to smack their toddler. Some people argue that it's wrong because, unlike other kinds of punishment, smacking is violent and abusive. But the truth is that shouting and screaming uncontrollably at a toddler can be just as abusive and emotionally scarring as an uncaring smack or slap.

The problem, in other words, goes deeper than smacking. It's about the way in which *any* punishment is given. There's a world of difference, for example, between tapping a toddler lightly on the wrist and giving a ten-year-old an angry slap or a prolonged thrashing with a belt. *Any* punishment given in an undisciplined way or in the heat of the moment is damaging. And, just as importantly, it won't work.　　　SEE CHAPTER 4

Temper Tantrums. Toddlers throw tantrums for four reasons: tiredness, frustration, rebellion or, most common of all, attention-seeking. If your toddler is bored and you're busy doing something else, you can almost guarantee they'll start misbehaving. If they can't get 'premium' attention, they'll settle for any form of attention they *can* get – even anger.

The way to deal with most tantrums is to *ignore bad behaviour* (unless it's dangerous or overly disruptive) and *praise good behaviour*. If your toddler is misbehaving because they want attention (rather than as a direct challenge), even telling them off is a way of rewarding that misbehaviour. They'll have gained your attention, which is what they were after, and, having learnt to do it success-fully, won't hesitate to use the same technique again in future. If you can ignore the tantrum, however, you'll be showing them it's an ineffective way to get your attention. When they finally realise it isn't working, they'll give up. Combine this with praising them for their self-control when they stop misbehaving.   SEE CHAPTER 4

Unconditional love. It's too soon for your toddler to have developed a healthy, objective self-image of their own, so they rely on you for all the love, support and affirmation they need. You're their main supplier of love and self-worth. If you show them as a toddler that they're a unique, valuable and highly prized person, they're likely to be happy whatever life throws at them. If not, they'll probably spend most of their lives searching for the love and acceptance they didn't feel they got from you. As their mum or dad, you have by far the biggest influence on them during their formative years, helping to shape their character for many years to come. The more you let them know, through words and actions, just how much you love them, the more likely they are to grow up happy, secure, self-confident and well-adjusted – in short, able to get the most out of life.   SEE CHAPTER 3

Video and TV. TV and films, and even CD-ROMs, can be a great source of entertainment and information for your toddler, sparking their imagination. Programmes like *Teletubbies* and *Sesame Street* can make them enthusiastic about learning; nature and wildlife shows can keep them enthralled and educated; and films and cartoons can provide *you* with a few well-deserved moments of peace and refreshment. But TV is passive, and your toddler needs active learning, so watch *with* your toddler, asking them simple questions about what they see and chatting with them about it the whole time it's on. TV can be used constructively as *part* of play, but it'll never be more than a minor resource. Your toddler won't learn what they need just by watching TV. They also need your help and encouragement, and lots and lots of time spent playing as actively and imaginatively as possible.   SEE CHAPTER 6

Walking. The typical toddler starts to walk at about thirteen months, though it can vary between seven and eighteen months. If you're worried or concerned, ask your GP to do a full assessment of what's called their 'gross motor' development. But bear in mind there's absolutely no evidence that a toddler who takes their time in stepping out will be anything but normal in later life. Sooner doesn't necessarily mean better. Don't expect your toddler to be that steady on their pegs for the first year or two. Expect them to fall over quite a bit. In order to walk well, they need muscle control, co-ordination, balance, concentration and visual depth perception. All this takes time and practice to acquire, so don't expect too much too soon, and make sure you give them plenty of praise when they do well.   SEE CHAPTER 5

X-rated. Secure families produce secure children, so if you have a partner, work hard to keep the romance alive in your relationship. Find times for the two of you to go out and enjoy yourselves. It's not pampering: it's survival! Don't be afraid to kiss or cuddle one another in front of your toddler. Knowing you love each other helps reassure them you love them too. And when the romance isn't there, continue to work hard at loving each other through all the arguments and hard times.

If you don't have a partner, it's still vital to find times to focus on your own needs. After all, a burnt-out parent is no good to an energy-obsessed toddler.   SEE CHAPTER 2

Yelling. According to the experts, only about 10 per cent of our communication is verbal. The words we use have less impact than how we say them and what we do. Yelling tells people that you're not calm, collected or in control, so don't yell at your toddler – it's more likely to under*mine* your authority than under*line* it. Most toddlers have acute hearing, so a quiet but firm command will work better than a frantic one. And don't be scared to confront your toddler – as a parent, *you're* the boss. Not only does your toddler not have the wisdom or experience to call the shots, they also need to know you're in charge for their own comfort. So take a deep breath – and speak calmly and with authority.   SEE CHAPTER 5

Zzzzzzzz! Sleep problems are very common with toddlers. Most wake up in the middle of the night at least once a week. Toddlers naturally go through sleep cycles of about one hour, waking or almost waking in between each cycle. This is only a problem if the reason they're waking is that they genuinely need comfort (due to teething, illness, bed-wetting or a nightmare), or if it disturbs the parents' sleep. In other words, it's usually a problem only if it's a problem for *you*. Sleep is a basic requirement for the body – the less disturbed it is, the better. So your aim is to stop them from waking you up in the middle of the night – it's better for both of you. Unless they're in real distress, ignore their cries as long as you can before going in and comforting them. If they regularly wake you up, try to cure them of the habit by gradually lengthening the period of time you take to respond to their cries.

Most toddlers need about twelve hours' sleep, though some can survive with less and younger toddlers will supplement their quota with one or two naps during the day. When setting bedtimes, try to build a consistent routine: work out what time you want them to wake up and count back from there. SEE CHAPTER 5

THE LAST WORD

The Navajo Indians of North America incorporate a kind of 'Marriage Race' into every wedding, as I found out a few years ago when I went to one. As part of the ceremony, all the women in the village run around its boundaries with the new bride. The bride finishes this 'race' first, with her immediate family – her mother, aunts and sisters – close behind, and all the other women just behind them. This isn't a tradition designed to ensure that all the women of the village get regular exercise. It's a powerful symbol of the way the Navajo recognise that we all need ongoing support from the whole community.

There was a time when you'd have known just where to turn for help in our society too. Uncles, aunts, parents, grandparents and great-grandparents all lived in the same village. They were on hand to offer useful and relevant guidance, support and baby-sitting when you needed it. But the family has shrunk considerably in the last century. Fifty years ago, your mother lived in the same street. A hundred years ago, she lived in the same house. Now you're lucky if she even lives in the same part of the country. Smaller families have given us independence, but at what cost? As extended families grow apart, we're becoming more and more isolated. Entire communities used to play a part in raising every child. Now we often feel as though we're out on our own, left to fend for ourselves.

But the truth is, you're *not* alone. Beyond this book, there are all sorts of resources available in the difficult, but rewarding, task of being a parent. From books and videos to courses and specialist organisations, help is literally only a phone call away. The next few pages give just an example of the kind of resources on offer, but for more information you can write to **Parentalk** at:

PO Box 23142, London, SE1 0ZT

Whatever you do, *don't* try to go it alone. You can be a great parent, so if you need help, get in touch.

FURTHER INFORMATION

Organisations

Parentalk
PO Box 23142
London SE1 0ZT

Tel: 0700 2000 500
Fax: 020 7450 9060
e-mail: info@parentalk.co.uk
Web site: www.parentalk.co.uk

Provides a range of resources and services designed to inspire parents to enjoy parenthood.

www.parentalkatwork.co.uk

A new web site for parents wanting to strike a healthy balance between work and family life. Parentalk at Work provides Top Tips, practical advice, discussion forums and links to other organisations.

Positive Parenting
1st floor
2A South Street
Gosport PO12 1ES

Tel: 023 9252 8787
Fax: 023 9250 1111
e-mail: info@parenting.org.uk
Web site: www.parenting.org.uk

Aims to prepare people for the role of parenting by helping parents, those about to become parents and also those who lead parenting groups.

Gingerbread
16–17 Clerkenwell Close
London EC1R 0AA

Tel: 020 7336 8183
Fax: 020 7336 8185
e-mail: office@gingerbread.org.uk
Web site: www.gingerbread.org.uk

Provides day-to-day support and practical help for lone parents.

Parentline Plus
520 Highgate Studios
53–76 Highgate Road
Kentish Town
London NW5 1TL

Helpline: 0808 800 2222
Fax: 020 7284 5501
e-mail:
      centraloffice@parentlineplus.org.uk
Web site: www.parentlineplus.org.uk

Provides freephone helpline called Parentline and courses for parents via the Parent Network Service.

Parentline Plus also includes the National Stepfamily Association. For all information call the Parentline freephone number on 0808 800 2222.

NSPCC
42 Curtain Road
London
EC2A 3NH

Helpline: 0800 800 500
Tel: 020 7825 2500
Fax: 020 7825 2525
Web site: www.nspcc.org.uk

Aims to prevent child abuse and neglect in all its forms and give practical help to families with children at risk. The NSPCC also produces leaflets with information and advice on positive parenting – call 020 7825 2500.

Care for the Family
PO Box 488
Cardiff
CF15 7YY

Tel: 029 2081 0800
Fax: 029 2081 4089
e-mail: care.for.the.family@cff.org.uk
Web site: www.care-for-the-family.org.uk

Provides support for families through seminars, resources and special projects.

Home-Start UK
2 Salisbury Road
Leicester LE1 7QR

Tel: 0116 2339955
Fax: 0116 2330232

e-mail: info@home-start.org.uk
Web site: www.home-start.org.uk

Volunteers offer support, friendship and practical help to young families in their own homes.

Kidscape
2 Grosvenor Gardens
London
SW1W 0DH

Helpline: 08451 205 204
Tel: 020 7730 3300
Fax: 020 7730 7081
e-mail: info@kidscape.org.uk
Web site: www.kidscape.org.uk

Works to prevent the abuse of children through education programmes involving parents and teachers, providing a range of resources. Also runs a bullying helpline.

Relate
Herbert Gray College
Little Church Street
Rugby
CV21 3AP

Tel: 01788 573241
e-mail:
                enquiries@national.relate.org.uk
Web site: www.relate.org.uk

Provides a confidential counselling service for relationship problems of any kind. Local branches are listed in the phone book.

180

Publications

The Sixty Minute Father, Rob Parsons, Hodder and Stoughton
How to Succeed as a Parent, Steve Chalke, Hodder and Stoughton
Positive Parenting: Raising Children with Self-Esteem, E. Hartley-Brewer,
    Mandarin Paperback
Raising Boys, Steve Biddulph, Thorsons
The Secret of Happy Children, Steve Biddulph, Thorsons
Families and How to Survive Them, Skinner and Cleese, Vermillion
Stress Free Parenting, Dr David Haslam, Vermillion
How Not to Be a Perfect Mother, Libby Purves, HarperCollins
Toddler Taming, Dr Christopher Green, Vermillion
Baby and Child: From Birth to Age Five, Penelope Leach, Penguin
What to Expect from the Toddler Years, Arlene Eisenberg, Heidi E. Murkoff
    and Sandee E. Hathaway, Simon and Schuster

Parenting Courses

- **Parentalk Parenting Course**
  A new parenting course designed to give parents the opportunity to share their
  experiences, learn from each other and discover some principles of parenting.
  Parentalk, PO Box 23142, London SE1 0ZT
  For more information phone 0700 2000 500
  e-mail: info@parentalk.co.uk
  Web site: www.parentalk.co.uk / www.parentalkatwork.co.uk

- **Parent Network**
  Operates through self-help groups run by parents for parents known as Parent-
  Link. The groups are mostly run for 2 or more hours, over 13 weekly sessions.
  For more information call **Parentline Plus** on 0808 800 2222.

- **Positive Parenting**
  Publishes a range of low cost, easy to read, common sense resource materials which
  provide help, information and advice. Responsible for running a range of parenting
  courses across the UK. For more information phone 023 9252 8787.

181

The **Paren**talk Parenting Course

Helping you to be a Better Parent

Being a parent is not easy. **Parentalk** is a new, video-led, parenting course designed to give groups of parents the opportunity to share their experiences, learn from each other and discover some principles of parenting. It is suitable for anyone who is a parent or is planning to become a parent.

The Parentalk Parenting Course features:

Steve Chalke – TV Presenter; author on parenting and family issues; father of four and **Parentalk** Founder.

Rob Parsons – author of *The Sixty Minute Father*; regular TV and radio contributor; and Executive Director of Care for the Family.

Dr Caroline Dickinson – inner city-based GP and specialist in obstetrics, gynaecology and paediatrics.

Kate Robbins – well-known actress and comedienne.

Each **Parentalk** session is packed with group activities and discussion starters.

Made up of eight sessions, the **Parentalk** Parenting Course is easy to use and includes everything you need to host a group of up to ten parents.

Each Parentalk Course Pack contains:
• A **Parentalk** Video
• Extensive, easy to use, group leader's guide
• Ten copies of the full-colour course material for members
• Photocopiable sheets/OHP masters

Price £49.95

Additional participant materials are available so that the course can be run again and again.

To order your copy, or to find out more, please contact:

Parentalk
PO Box 23142, London SE1 0ZT
Tel: 020 7450 9072 *or* 020 7450 9073
Fax: 020 7450 9060
e-mail: info@parentalk.co.uk